Inspiration
for a Woman's Soul:™
CHOOSING
HAPPINESS

Compiled by Linda Joy • *Edited by Bryna René*

Published by Inspired Living Publishing, LLC.
P.O. Box 1149, Lakeville, MA 02347

ISBN-13: 978-0-9845006-4-2
ISBN-10: 0-9845006-4-2

Library of Congress Control Number: 2014922230

www.InspiredLivingPublishing.com
(508) 265-7929

Cover and Layout Design: Rachel Dunham, www.YourBrandTherapy.com

Editor: Bryna René, Aphrodite, Inc. www.wordsbyaphrodite.com

Printed in the United States.

Choosing Happiness

Dedication

This book is dedicated to ...

Every woman who bravely chooses happiness for herself in the midst of life's messiness.

Every woman who reaches with an outstretched hand to uplift, empower, and support other women on the path of self-discovery.

Every woman who chooses honesty over fear, authenticity over presentation, and love over separation.

And also to ...

Niki, my beautiful daughter: you inspire me with your wide-open heart, loving compassion, and beautiful soul. I am honored beyond words that you were gifted to me in this lifetime. Watching you with your daughter is one of the greatest blessings in my life.

Makenna (aka "The Little Goddess"), my spirited three-year-old granddaughter: you took my heart by storm, and reminded me that joy and happiness are within reach whenever we allow ourselves to be fully in the moment. May the world always embrace your magnificence, my love, and never dull your sparkle.

Tyler, my grandson, the "other man" in my life: you continue to inspire me with your loving, compassionate heart, and your quest to find fairness and balance in the world around you. May you always remain true to who you are, and find the greatest peace and happiness in that truth.

Dana, my soul mate, best friend, love of my life: twenty years in, you still make my heart skip a beat, bring a smile to my lips, and make me feel like the most important woman in the world. I give thanks every day that you're my man.

The multitude of extraordinary women who have come into my life over the last twenty five years, whether for a moment or a lifetime: your brilliant spirits have touched and inspired me beyond words. My greatest wish is that I might light the way for others as you have for me.

My coauthors, who have trusted me to share their intimate stories with the world. Your bravery through the sometimes-painful writing process continues to inspire me.

The extraordinary team of women with whom I have been honored, blessed, and humbled to work to bring this project to life: Bryna René, Editor for Inspired Living Publishing, who brings the essence of each story to light with ease and grace; Rachel Dunham, the creative branding visionary behind the visual graphics of this book (and all my brands), who continues to amaze me with her innate gifts; my beyond-extraordinary assistant Nichol Skaggs, who keeps it all running smoothly; and Kim Turcotte, my Web Project Manager, who brings my online visions to life.

And finally, to ...

You, the reader—the beautiful, deserving recipient of the love and light in these pages. I am humbled by gratitude for your choice to share in this creation. May you always find what your soul is seeking.

Praise for
CHOOSING
HAPPINESS

"You deserve to be wildly happy, and happiness comes down to powerful choices more than circumstances. These stories provide true examples of finding our mojo and turning our lives around, one choice at a time."
— **Tama Kieves**, best-selling author of *This Time I Dance! Creating the Work You Love, Inspired & Unstoppable: Wildly Succeeding in Your Life's Work*, and *A Year without Fear*

"We don't always choose the hand we are dealt, but we can choose how we move forward as we play the hand amidst adversity and change. The inspiring stories in Inspiration for a Woman's Soul: Choosing Happiness will ignite you and show you that choosing happiness is a way to move forward in life."
— **Kristine Carlson**, coauthor of the New York Times best-selling book series *Don't Sweat the Small Stuff*

"The riveting stories in this book are living proof of the mystical power behind our choice to be happy. When we live and breathe joy into even the most difficult life challenges, we magically undo misfortune and link into the alchemy of happiness. This book and the stories within it offer hope for those who struggle to find this treasure."
— **Cindy L. Heath**, author of *Real Beautiful: The Secret Energy of the Mind, Body, & Spirit*

"Linda Joy has done it again with her newest book … This book reminds you to claim the happiness that is rightfully yours. As each story reveals, no matter what your circumstances, all you have to do is make the choice! *You* get to choose happiness, and you start by reading this book!"
— **Terri Britt**, award-winning author of *The Enlightened Mom*, Inspirational Speaker, and former Miss USA 1982

"Linda has truly created a masterpiece. She has collected powerful, inspirational, and deeply personal stories that left me not only touched, but motivated to be a better woman. These authors are incredible storytellers and their vulnerability is beautiful. I was so inspired by Linda's story, as well as by how all of the [authors] have consciously chosen to live with joy, no matter what they've been through!"
– **Erin Cox**, Business Strategist for enlightened entrepreneurs and author of *One Hot Mama: The Guide to Getting Your Mind and Body Back After Baby.*

"When you choose to live life on your terms, you feel empowered and joyful, peaceful and accomplished. Linda Joy's *Choosing Happiness* illuminates the poignant moments in these women's lives … and what authentic happiness truly is. Thank you for sharing these incredible stories!"
– **Jackie Ruka**, America's Happyologist and author of *Get Happy and Create a Kick-Butt Life! A Creative Toolbox to Rapidly Activate the Life You Desire.*

"I am grateful to these courageous women for revealing the challenges they faced while making the deliberate choice to show up as their most powerful, purposeful selves. Written like private conversations, these stories will inspire you in two ways. First, their authenticity and vulnerability will motivate you to show up in your own life. Second, the journaling questions will entice you towards a deeper level of personal wisdom, understanding, and unspeakable joy!"
– **Adrienne Fikes**, the Soul Power Coach™ and Creator of the 30-Second Soul Power Challenge™

"*Inspiration for a Woman's Soul: Choosing Happiness* truly is inspiration for *any* soul. These stories of courage, wisdom, and transformation will touch your heart, inspire your mind, heal your sadness, and light up your life. Knowing that others have gone through the fire, overcome the fear, and seen the gift within is a beautiful thing. Bestselling inspirational publisher Linda Joy has hit it out of the park again!"
– **Debra Oakland**, founder of LivinginCourage.com

"*Inspiration for a Woman's Soul: Choosing Happiness* is a refreshing compilation … Touching, inspiring and even a bit emotional, this book is a great read if you feel stuck in achieving your goals or need a little boost from others who have been there too. Highly recommended, beautifully done!"
– **Dina Proctor**, best-selling author of *Madly Chasing Peace: How I Went from Hell to Happy in 9 Minutes a Day*

"There is something extraordinary happening: modern women are evolving and growing at a rate never before seen! In this book, twenty-seven female thought leaders reveal astonishingly personal tragedies and triumphs. Yet even more importantly, they share the soul growth and clarity that arrives to them as they move through these experiences. Vulnerable, emotional, conscious, and very, very inspiring!"
– **Sara Wiseman,** author and founder of Intuition University

"*Inspiration for a Woman's Soul: Choosing Happiness* redefines what it means to be rich—rich in clarity, rich in love, rich in happiness, and rich in purpose. The women whose voices shine from these pages are survivors, as are we all. I recognized myself in their stories, and as they shared their journeys back from those pivotal moments when they knew something had to change, I found myself cheering their successes. The strategies and perspectives they share are both helpful and inspiring. A beautiful book to be savored and shared."
– **Susan Lander, Esq.,** author of *Conversations with History: Inspiration, Reflections and Advice from History-Makers and Celebrities on the Other Side*

"The choice to live happy is sacred to my heart. In *Choosing Happiness*, the amazing authors have shared stories that speak directly to my soul. The road to satisfaction can have many twists and turns, but the journeys these authors share are truly inspirational. This is a book of soul-inspiring secrets, gently guiding you to discover your true path to happiness, bliss, and ultimate fulfillment. Once I started reading, I simply couldn't put it down."
– **Bailey Frumen, MSW, LCSW,** Psychotherapist & Lifestyle Design Coach

"Linda Joy has masterfully compiled a mosaic of life-lesson gems that sparkle with unique clarity and brilliance. Each candid story in *Choosing Happiness* leads to grander self-awareness, and to the beautiful place where happiness lives and flourishes. I connected deeply to each author as I delved into their revelations, darkest shadows, and celebrated victories. Relatable! Real! Life-changing!"
– **Kellie R. Stone,** international best-selling author, founder of Women's LifeLink, and Women's Life Purpose Visionary

"The dream team has done it again! Something beautiful happens when courageous souls open their hearts and share their stories—and there is a story in here for everyone. Reading, you can't help but think to yourself 'Wow! That is *so* me!' This book is easy to relate to and will create awakenings for a lot of women. Truly warm and inspiring."
– **Gina Hussar,** author, Happiness Coach, and Creator of the 6 Month Miracle Project

"I was introduced to *Choosing Happiness* at the perfect time! A sudden emergency showed up in my life, but this book helped me stay in a much better mindset. In each story, there are nuggets of inspiration, hope, and wisdom, and profound reminders that we *do* have a choice in how we perceive things, and that we can create our own happiness."
– **Maryellen De Vine,** Life Coach and Angelic EFT Practitioner

"The inspiring stories from these amazing authors prove that happiness in life is a choice. The valuable lessons given by each author leave the reader with a feeling of hope, love—and, of course, happiness. *Choosing Happiness* is a reflection of each author's heart and soul, and will guide every reader to find her own life's purpose and destiny. This book is a must-read for anyone searching for more happiness and joy!"
– **Kellie Poulsen-Grill,** Happiness Expert, retreat facilitator, and best-selling author

"*Inspiration for a Woman's Soul: Choosing Happiness* is a book that shares strength, empowerment, and special wisdom in stories that will warm your heart and transform your life. These powerful stories from the hearts of real women transform Choice, Letting Go, Freedom, Forgiveness, Healing, Connection, and Loving Yourself into sacred journeys. This book gives you new opportunities to embrace your own journey and feel the power of inspiration that is guiding your life, right now."
– **Lumari,** Intuitive Guide & Coach, Visionary Energy Master, Transformational Healer and best-selling author

"Awakening, growing in consciousness, and embracing the ever-present happiness within us is possible! Please allow these stories to guide you toward that happiness."
– **Dr. Jennifer Howard,** author of the best-selling, multiple-award-winning book, *Your Ultimate Life Plan: How to Deeply Transform Your Everyday Experience and Create Changes That Last*

"One of the best ways to learn how to move into your personal power and joy is to read about how others do it. You will be profoundly inspired by these wise and courageous women as they share their challenging journeys with you. Don't miss reading *Inspiration for a Woman's Soul: Choosing Happiness*."
– **Margaret Paul, PhD,** cocreator of Inner Bonding, author/coauthor of *Do I Have To Give Up Me To Be Loved By You?*, *Healing Your Aloneness*, *Inner Bonding*, and *Do I Have To Give Up Me To Be Loved By God?*

"In the depth of despair, how do you move past pain's gridlock or step out of the darkness? Inspired Living Publisher Linda Joy offers an inspiring new book of courageous stories with one theme: Choosing Happiness. Learn why happiness matters ... Twenty-seven authors have completed the journey, and now offer you the opportunity to grow through their elegant stories."
– **Dr. Caron Goode, NCC,** founder, HeartWise® Life and Academy for Coaching Parents International

Foreword
by Shannon Kaiser

*L*ast week, someone asked me if I would still do the work I do today if I won the lottery. I answered with a resounding "Yes!"

In most respects, I feel like I have already won the lottery. I wake up every morning incredibly excited to live out a new day. I get to do work I love and make a great living as an author, teacher, life coach, and speaker. I am in love with myself, my body and my life. I am beyond happy.

But it wasn't always this way.

Several years ago, I was diagnosed with clinical depression. At the time, I was also suffering from eating disorders and drug addictions. My relationships were toxic. I hated my corporate job and walked around like a shell of a human being. I was alive, but barely living.

The world told me to go to a good school, get great grades, land a great job in a city you love, and find a man to settle down with. That was the golden ticket to happiness. So there I was, with all of what society said would make me happy—but I was crying hysterically on the cold bathroom floor.

I yelled out, "I can't do this anymore. I can't keep pretending to be someone I am not!" In an instant, the air around me thinned out, my tears dried up, and a calm presence filled the room. I heard my inner voice chime, "Shannon, follow your heart."

I realized, in that moment, that the pain, chaos, and depression were happening in part because I was *allowing* it. I was focused on what wasn't working and drowning in my own sorrow. I spent too much time consumed with how bad things were, instead of carving out space to think about what I wanted, or how good things might be.

That bathroom breakdown was a turning point in my life. I realized I had only two choices: I could continue to allow my depression to run my life and be alive but not live, or I could choose to follow my heart.

Over the next several years, I did just that. When I acknowledged myself and what I needed for myself, real, authentic happiness finally became attainable.

As Linda Joy explains in her introduction, happiness is cultivated from within. We have to look at the areas of our life that aren't working before we can step into a life we love. The contrast brings clarity.

Once you choose happiness, your entire life shifts. Your relationships become less strained. You make healthier choices. You are more present. The things you want come to you faster. Most importantly, you begin to fall in love with yourself and your life.

This book will help you get there.

As a six-time contributing author to the *Chicken Soup for the Soul* Series, I understand the tremendous value of short stories shared from the heart. The book in your hands is a collection of stories from women just like me and you. They have traveled to the emotional depths of the human spirit to find what they needed all along: themselves.

Linda Joy (publisher of this book and the other anthologies in this series) is both a spiritual teacher and inspirational catalyst. Fueled by passion, she is on a mission to create a world where everyone is choosing happiness and joy. Everything she puts out into the world is about empowerment—specifically, empowering *you* to make a choice and stand up to live your great life.

Linda created this book as a guide to help us see the light in the darkness. She has found an eloquent way to break down the process of choosing happiness, mining the gold in these powerful stories and giving us a recipe to follow in our own lives.

The book is broken up into chapters, each cleverly designed to be a blueprint for feeling good. First, you must make a choice to be happy (Chapter One). Once you do, you move into letting go (Chapter Two). This process leads to an expansive freedom (Chapter Three), which then opens your heart to forgiveness (Chapter Four). The healing process comes full circle (Chapter Five), and you are open to connecting with other like-minded people (Chapter Six). Ultimately, the journey to happiness and living your dream life comes back to loving yourself unconditionally (Chapter Seven).

The wonderful women who share their stories in this precious book have found happiness through this blueprint—women like Peggy Nolan, who at age forty was diagnosed with cancer but chose to embrace her passionate love for life, or Mal Duane, whose alcohol-induced rock bottom connected her with her highest purpose. At one point or another, every woman in this book (including myself) felt like happiness was an impossible experience. But choosing happiness is not about living a life free of setbacks or pain. It's about learning to see the purpose in all of life's moments. High or low, we can always choose joy—and today, we are living happy lives that far exceed our old expectations.

Unlike other books of short stories, *Choosing Happiness* invites you to go deeper with Reflection Questions at the end of each section. You are invited to become an active participant in your own journey to lasting happiness. Please take time to allow the words of each story to soak into your soul. As you answer each journaling question, your life will transform.

Congratulations! Your happiest life starts now. By picking up this book you have said, "I am worth it, and my dreams matter!" You are now part of the collective sisterhood of women who come together to show our raw, vulnerable, beautiful selves. With each transformational story, you will see that happiness is possible for you, too. It is only a choice away.

Choose love. Choose life. Choose *happy*. And soon, you too will feel like every day is a lottery-winning day.

Shannon Kaiser
The Joy Guru
Bestselling author of *Find Your Happy: An Inspirational Guide to Loving Life to Its Fullest*

TABLE OF
Contents

Introduction

by Linda Joy, *Publisher*

On a spring day in 1991, I discovered the healing power of choice.

My life, and my soul's work, began that day, as I sobbed against my steering wheel on the side of a tree-lined road. As I cried out to the Universe for help, I was given an epiphany. I could choose to continue as I was—a welfare mom, a victim of my traumatic past, a woman without hope for her own future—or I could choose something different.

That beautiful, sacred truth—that I have a *choice* about how I experience my life—filled my heart with hope and forever changed the trajectory of my life. Today, it continues to fuel my work as the publisher and host of numerous media brands (including *Aspire Magazine*) which are dedicated to inspiring women to live deeper, more deliberate, more authentic lives.

Through this amazing work which I'm blessed to do, I've met and heard from thousands of extraordinary women who have created authentic, joyful, inspiring lives for themselves and their families. While these women have each traveled their own unique paths, and overcome their own pain, obstacles, and perceived failures, their stories still seem to have a common thread. At some point in her life, each woman made a pivotal choice of some kind, a conscious decision that changed her life and her own role within it.

Every day, in every moment, we have the ability to choose happiness. Even in the midst of the darkest night, when everything is falling apart, that choice is still available. Sometimes, it's not until we hit rock bottom that we see the choice before us—but sometimes, all it takes is a gentle reminder that we are powerful, lovable, and worthy enough to create our lives and ourselves in the image of the Divine and according to our souls' plans.

The stories in this book are the soul-inspiring truths of women who have been there, done that, and come out the other side in a blaze of light. Utilizing the authentic storytelling model that is the heart of our mission at Inspired Living Publishing, these twenty-seven authors have banished their fears about speaking their truth, gone deep into their souls, and offered up their stories as healing tools for *you*. My hope is that you will see some part of yourself in them, and understand that the empowered choices these ladies have made are yours to make as well.

Happiness, joy, love, and inspired living are yours for the taking. All you have to do is choose!

Wishing you love, happiness, and divine inspiration!

Linda Joy

PS: If you're curious and would like the in-depth version of my personal story, you can find it in my first anthology through Inspired Living Publishing, *A Juicy Joyful Life* (2010).

Chapter
One

Happiness is ...
Making a Choice

Not Afraid to Live

Peggy Nolan

"Are you always this happy?" she asked.

I sat on the edge of the exam table in my oncologist's office. The freelance writer in the chair across from me was following my doctor around for the day, interviewing selected patients for an article in *SELF* Magazine.

I smiled at her. At forty, I'd barely made the cut to be interviewed as a "young" woman diagnosed with breast cancer.

"I mean," she continued, "What makes you so different from the last woman I interviewed?"

"Different? What do you mean?"

"She's your age, same diagnosis. Same treatment. But she's terribly depressed and angry."

"Hmm." I couldn't think what to say next.

She interrupted my silence. "Let's start with your hair. Do you wear a wig?"

I laughed. "No. Wigs are itchy."

"Do you cover up or try to hide the fact that you're bald?"

"Oh, *heck* no. That takes too much time!"

"So losing your hair doesn't bother you?"

"Honey, I don't have to shave. Anywhere."

She blinked, confused. "What do you mean?"

Hadn't she seen me wink? "I don't have to shave my legs or my armpits. I don't need to wax my eyebrows, or my lip, or my pubic area."

Her face flushed a deep red. "Oh." She scribbled something in her note pad. "But really, it doesn't bother you?"

I paused and took a deep breath. So much for my sense of humor. "I lost my breast," I told her. "My hair will grow back."

"Right," she said, biting her lip. "What about work, then? Do you still work full time?"

"Absolutely."

She scribbled again in her note pad. "I don't get it," she mumbled. "What makes you so different from the last lady?"

I thought about that for a moment. "At some point," I said slowly, "I realized I had a choice. I could be bitter and pissed off that I have cancer, or I could embrace life in all its messiness and wonderfulness, and be happy."

The writer gaped at me as though I had three heads. "And what point was that?"

* * * * * *

For my fortieth birthday, my gynecologist sent me for my baseline mammogram. It never dawned on me that something would not be right—but sure enough, the next morning I got a call telling me I needed to see a surgeon. My mammogram showed a suspiciously large microcalcification cluster. After a biopsy and a round of second and third opinions at Dana Farber Cancer Institute, my diagnosis was confirmed: Invasive Breast Cancer.

I remember drowning my fear in a vodka martini. I remember the dreadful phone call to my parents. I remember thinking "I could die from this." How would I tell my teenage daughters, Jessica and Christina? What could I possibly say to them?

I remember that I broke the news while we were watching "Under the Tuscan Sun." I told my girls what I knew about my condition, and that I needed surgery. I reassured them that my doctors were absolutely certain they'd caught my cancer early, and that I'd be fine.

I wasn't sure they believed me. I wasn't sure *I* believed me.

I remember lying in my bed, crying as quietly as I could, thinking about what life would look like after I was gone. I needed to find a good lawyer who could help me get my affairs in order. What little I had belonged to my girls, not my ex-husband.

My girls ... Thinking of Christina made me cry even harder. I wasn't finished with her yet. At sixteen, she still needed me to be there for her. She still needed Mom.

I tossed in bed. Should I bother my oldest daughter? Should I cry in front of her? I tiptoed down the hall and knocked on her bedroom door.

"Come in," she said.

Her blue eyes were puffy. I could tell she'd been crying, too. Jessica wrapped her arms around me and I laid my head in her lap. "I don't know what to say," she said.

"Just let me cry."

"You can't die, mom," her stoic voice didn't quite hide her fear.

"I know."

What scared me most was dying before Christina turned eighteen, before she graduated from high school, before Jessica graduated from college.

It shook me to my core to think of dying before wedding dress shopping, or holding my grandbabies for the first time. Before knowing what it feels like to have a man truly, madly, deeply love me, and to feel the same way about him. Before seeing the Grand Canyon, the Scottish Highlands, or the Aurora Borealis.

I didn't want to die. I wasn't ready to die. I could still make a difference.

As I prepared for surgery to remove not just the cancer but my left breast and twenty-six lymph nodes, I had my living will and health care wishes notarized. It struck me as funny that I needed someone to witness me sign my life away. As I stepped out of the town clerk's office, an amazing, warm calm flooded through my being. The world around me seemed to stand still. The sky was bluer, the grass greener. The birds seemed to sing directly to me.

I had just looked the worst possible outcome in the face. I could die. Breast cancer could kill me. Now, with the loose ends of my last wishes neatly wrapped up and filed away, there was nothing left for me to do but live. And I mean *really* live.

From that day forward, I no longer sought the approval of others. I no longer feared being rejected. I gave up blaming my ex-husband for the demise of our marriage, and forgave him and myself. I gave up complaining about other people. I gave up perfectionism, diet soda, and fast food.

I decided to own my life and take responsibility for every one of my choices and decisions. I didn't have a set of directions to follow, so I fumbled around a lot, and made a lot of mistakes. "Three steps forward, two steps backwards is still progress," I'd remind myself. Living in a way that left no room for regret, I was able to make peace with my pieces and embrace my wonderfully messy life.

Most of all, I chose to be happy, and do things that made me happy.

Two weeks after my mastectomy, I went to see David Bowie in concert with my girlfriends.

Seven weeks after my mastectomy, I took my girls to Playa del Carmen, Mexico with my mom and my sister. I visited ancient Mayan ruins and (despite my unreasonable fear of falling) climbed the great Mayan pyramid. The view from the top was breathtaking.

When chemo caused my hair to fall out in clumps, I invited family and friends to my head-shaving party. Throughout my bald phase, I didn't wear a wig or a scarf, but proudly showed off my smooth scalp (and legs and underarms). In 2004, while I was undergoing radiation therapy, the Red Sox won the World Series. Christina claimed it was because she rubbed my bald head for luck before every game.

When Christina graduated and moved out, I settled in to enjoy being an empty-nester with my two dogs. That's when my truly, madly, deeply finally found me. In 2006, I married the man of my dreams—who just happened to be my first boyfriend from high school. He graced me with four children from his first marriage and an amazing extended family. Since then, I've watched three of my four beautiful daughters get married, and have been blessed with my first two grandchildren.

In 2007 I started Muay Thai Kickboxing, something I never would have tried in a million years before my diagnosis. Today, I'm a second degree black belt. In 2010 I received my certification to teach yoga. These two wildly different yet similar disciplines keep my physical and emotional being happy and healthy.

While I have yet to hike the Scottish Highlands or island-hop through Greece, I have been to Italy, Spain, Ireland, Bermuda, Mexico, the Grand Canyon, the Turks and Caicos, Key West, Florida, and many other amazing places. Travel makes my heart sing. Visiting interesting places beyond my backyard fulfills the promise I made to myself when I chose to live.

Eleven years ago, I had trouble articulating to that freelance writer why I was so different from the angry patient she interviewed before me. I didn't know how to describe my choice to be happy without the experience to back it up. I wish I could look her up today, and tell her exactly what makes me different, because I know now what it is.

I'm not afraid to live.

Reflection Questions

If you found out you were going to die one year from today, what would you want to do with your life? How can you bring those experiences into your life right now?

_____

_____

_____

_____

What would your life look and feel like if you no longer feared your worst-case scenario?

_____

_____

_____

Peggy's positive attitude played a big part in her recovery from cancer. Where can you shift your own perception to see the positive side of a tough situation?

_____

_____

_____

The Choice That Changed My Life

Boni Lonnsburry

*I*t was the worst year *ever.*

It began with my father visiting for the holidays. He didn't seem himself; he was grumpy, tired and impatient, and you could tell he didn't feel well. When he called soon after he returned home to Florida I wasn't all that surprised to learn he'd been diagnosed with lung cancer. Six months later, he was gone.

That same year, my divorce was finalized. After sixteen years of marriage I was carving a new life for myself as a single woman. I knew it was the right thing, but still, it was unknown territory: scary, uncomfortable, and challenging.

My two teenage sons had been acting out, so I begrudgingly allowed them to move in with their dad. Two weeks later I received a letter from his lawyer announcing that they would be moving across the country that week. My heart broke.

And, as if the emotional burdens weren't difficult enough, my finances were a train wreck. My house was in foreclosure, I had no job, and now that child support had ended, so had my sole source of income. I was failing miserably at a multi-level marketing program and spending every cent I had for leads that I could not, for the life of me, convert to sales.

I pulled the curtains, shut out the world, and ignored the phone (which rang incessantly, always with creditors wanting to be paid). I wanted to disappear. How did I get to be so broke, sad, and hopeless? I was "spiritual," after all—I even knew about the Law of Attraction! Why couldn't I get my life together and create something better than this constant struggle?

I don't remember the exact day it happened. I *do* remember waking up and feeling good for a moment. Then my sad state of affairs came to mind, and the familiar feelings of fear, powerlessness, and futility settled back into their usual places.

I dragged myself out of bed and made my morning cup of mocha. As I sat curled up in a chair with a warm comforter pulled around me, sipping my delicious brew, it dawned on me: right this very minute everything was fine. I was warm, fed, and sheltered. A beautiful day was dawning outside my window, my kids were safe, my cat was curled up on my lap … Why did I have to go back to feeling bad?

That question stunned me. Why indeed, did I have to go back to feeling bad? The smart-ass, negative me piped up, "Because, you idiot, your life is a shambles!"

But for once, I didn't listen to her. Instead, I thought to myself. "Yes, my life could be better, but it also could be a hell of a lot worse. I'm healthy and smart—why, I even have some wisdom! Why am I focusing on how terrible everything is and letting that determine my emotional state?"

And from that moment on, I made The Choice. Maybe I couldn't do anything about my dad dying, the divorce, the foreclosure, or my kids moving to New York, but I *could* choose how I felt, despite all of those things. There was no reason on earth why I couldn't be happy *now*. I was sick and tired of feeling bad, so I decided to choose "happy" instead.

"I'd rather be a happy bag lady living on the streets than an unhappy anything else," I thought.

What I didn't realize is that The Choice would rock my world and change everything in it.

Oh, it wasn't easy at first. My habit was to fall headfirst into self-pity at the drop of a hat. I had to train myself to focus on the positive. I had to stay firmly planted in the present moment. Thinking about the bills and wondering if I'd have to live in my car were not happiness-producing thoughts. So, I'd focus on what was happening at each "now" moment—I called it "narrowing my focus"—and it worked.

"Right now, I am alive, healthy, and enjoying a delicious dinner at a friend's house," I would think. "In this moment all is well, and I am happy."

In time, The Choice gave me a gift even greater than freedom from unhappiness. It actually reset my emotions and gave me the freedom to choose different thoughts, which resulted in different feelings, and, not too long later, different realties.

Once I decided "happy first," it didn't seem to matter that I didn't have money and was soon to lose my home. I knew that, even if the worst did happen, I'd figure out something. I began to pay more attention to what I *did* have, and to feel grateful for the little things.

I also began a little ritual. Each morning, I would sit for five minutes, close my eyes, and imagine myself at a riverside café in the south of France. My Higher Self sat at this table with me, as did my subconscious mind (personified) and my Future Self (the one who had it all together). Sipping café au lait in the Riviera sun, the four of us would "intend" the day.

I would speak to my other Selves about what I wanted to experience that day, emotionally. "I want to feel excited today!" I'd exclaim. "I want to feel joyous and prosperous, and have fun. I want to feel as if I am making a positive difference."

I would then *feel* how each of those feelings felt, so my team would know what I really meant. I had spent years saying I intended to feel great, but feeling awful instead; I wanted them to know the difference.

Once the parameters for the day were established, my Higher Self agreed, my subconscious mind changed any opposing beliefs, and my Future Self assured me I would love the day to come.

And I did.

My life began to change in little ways at first. I landed a job as a temp within two weeks of The Choice. It didn't pay much—only $10 an hour—but it was more than I'd made in a very long time.

I remember the first check I received from the temp job: it was for $164. My rent was $1000, so it wasn't going to go far. But instead of worrying about that, I forced myself to feel grateful. I told myself, "Yesterday you didn't have this $164. Today you do. *You* created this abundance in your life." And suddenly, I felt as grateful as if the check were for a million dollars.

Within a month, I had a full time job offer from one of the temp jobs. It was fun and exciting, paid great, and allowed me to feel like I was making a difference. It wasn't my own company, which was my ultimate dream, but it was a great step in the direction of prosperity.

I continued my daily ritual, and made The Choice each and every day. Okay, yes, sometimes I fell off the happy wagon into worry and doubt. I sought to control my circumstances rather than let them unfold magically. But I'd gotten used to feeling great every day, and those negative feelings felt worse than ever. Each and every time, I pulled myself out of the pits and back into happiness— and each time, I shed another of the beliefs that had kept me hog-tied to scarcity. Lo and behold, my world began to shift in even bigger ways.

I was offered a job as a Vice President at a startup company and—get this—*I was given a percentage of the company!* I owned (at least a little bit) of my own company! My dream was coming true.

I worked my tail off: morning, noon, and night, and every weekend for six months. I had so much fun. Every day was filled with excitement.

Then, the company went under.

But, as I'd learned in the past few years, bad news doesn't always mean bad news. "I wonder what will happen now?" I thought. Part of me didn't even care. I was *happy*. Nothing could take that away.

Because I wasn't attached to the outcome, I was totally open when the solution presented itself. My boss approached me and said, "Why don't we start our own marketing company with some of the same clients? You could run it from your home and I'll be the silent partner!"

We each invested $50 for the incorporation. She helped me line up two part-time gigs as well, and I worked at all three jobs, having the time of my life. Not much money was coming in, but I loved the adventure, freedom, and fun of choosing my own hours and working from home.

Meanwhile, I continued my morning ritual. Within six months, I bought my partner out. Within five years, and without investing another dime, my company was grossing $5 million a year.

In the years since I made The Choice, my life has become more and more of a fairy tale. I have abundance beyond my wildest dreams, a deeply loving relationship, travel, adventure, and a multitude of successes.

Have these things made me happier? Well, they've certainly *added* to my happiness. But the interesting thing is, I still make The Choice. I've discovered that, if I look hard enough, there is always something to feel bad about—and the inverse is true as well. Happiness is a choice I make every single day, and it always pays off. Yes, it feels great, but more importantly, it helps to create even more wonderful realities.

The Choice is powerful. The Choice plus a dream (and the knowledge of how to create it) are *exponentially* powerful!

Reflection Questions

Boni first learned how to be happy by feeling gratitude in the present moment. What past or future thoughts are you holding on to? Do these contribute to your happiness, or work against it?

_____

_____

_____

_____

What is your daily ritual for staying in touch with your higher self?

_____

_____

_____

_____

What apparent setbacks in your life have turned into gifts?

_____

_____

_____

_____

What Happens When Your Heart Breaks Open

Mal Duane

I remember December 30, 1988 as if it were yesterday.

I was curled up in a ball, wearing my favorite flannel leopard print pajamas, with the covers pulled over my head. My face was bloated, my eyes red and swollen, and I had a splitting headache from all the alcohol I had drunk earlier in the day. The room was pitch black, blinds closed; the only noise was my sniffling as I cried.

I was hitting my bottom.

I thought about dying. How wonderful it would be to leave the black hole I had been living in! My alcoholism and depression had taken over the last shred of my ripped-apart life. The wounds of my catastrophic divorce from another alcoholic were still raw, and I was drowning my broken heart. It wasn't the first time: I had a habit of attaching myself to unlikely partners who would ultimately leave me in the most gut-wrenching ways. I was dying a very slow death, emotionally and physically, and I knew with certainty that I didn't have it in me to continue on this path for one more day. I couldn't face the New Year.

I began to pray, silently. *Dear God, how do I end this now, once and for all?*

The thought of death brought relief. No more struggling with my drinking, or the failed relationships that kept tearing my heart out.

Maybe I should just take a handful of Xanax and end this, I thought.

And then, I heard a voice, so clear that it startled me. "Oh, dear child, you can't leave now!"

I peeked over the covers to see if there was someone there—but the room was still dark and empty.

The voice continued, "You have much work to do. You have many lessons to learn, and when you have mastered those lessons, you will need to go and teach others. You have an amazing life ahead of you, and much to do on my behalf."

Was I having a nervous breakdown? I scanned the room again. I couldn't tell if the voice was in my head, or if someone else was present, hiding in the shadows while they spoke to me. I pulled the covers up over my head once more, but that didn't keep the voice out.

"Child, fear not. It is time to put an end to your suffering."

With those words, an unexplainable feeling of peace came over me. My fear dropped away. I knew in that instant that I wasn't crazy; I was having a spiritual awakening after a long, dark night of the soul. My heart had broken open, and for the first time the light of God was able to touch me.

My first thought was, *why am I being saved?* What could I possibly give to others? I knew only self-condemnation and destructive behaviors.

I turned the lights on and ran into the bathroom to make sure nothing had happened to me—but the swollen face, red eyes, and runny nose were still there, and my head was still pounding from the nasty hangover. Yet, I felt different.

Holding onto the sink, I looked into the mirror. For the first time in a very long time, I wasn't disgusted by what I saw. There was a sadness in my watery eyes that spoke to me. *What have you been doing to yourself, girl?* I thought. *It's time to get off this path of chaos and destruction. I will help you now.*

At the break of day, I got dressed and ran to my neighbor George's house. George was a sponsor in Alcoholics Anonymous, and was understandably surprised to see me standing on his doorstep! At first he acted very coolly towards me (probably thinking I was looking for a drink), but it didn't take long for him to feel my sincerity. For months, he'd been telling me that he was holding a chair for me at the meetings, and this New Year's Eve morning, I told him that I was ready to sit in it.

I started 1989 as a sober woman. Twenty-six years later, I am still in recovery.

Once I got sober, my life started to transform dramatically. I discovered a burning desire to learn more about spirituality and personal development. I read everything I could get my hands on from Wayne Dyer, Louise Hay, and *A Course in Miracles*. I started a daily meditation practice, and got on my knees morning and night to thank God and ask him to relieve me of the bondage of myself. What I learned about our own individual power to transform our lives provoked me to dig deeper. I began to discover my value as a kind and loving woman. The things that made me unique were not burdens or flaws, but my greatest gifts. Being six feet tall was not a deformity. Wanting to be loved was normal. My value as a person was not based on my past mistakes, but on what I was doing right now to care for myself and help others.

I embraced recovery early on, and never really thought much about alcohol again, which is highly unusual. But once the physical effects of my alcohol abuse subsided, I realized that I had other issues to work on besides my addiction. With my mind clear, I was able to look at my life with a far more rational view. I realized I had damaged every relationship in my life, and while the razor-sharp sword of self-condemnation was stabbing me less and less, there was still a deep sense of shame I needed to heal from.

When I started my recovery, there was still a stigma about being a woman and an alcoholic, but over time, the negativity lessened as women like Betty Ford, Elizabeth Taylor, and Jamie Lee Curtis opened up about their personal struggles with addiction.

Betty Ford became my personal hero. As one of the most recognized faces in the world, she could have chosen to hide her addiction from the public. Instead, she bravely attended AA meetings, opened a treatment facility, and was a pioneer in getting help for addicts. In 2011, just before she died, I sent her a copy of my book and received a personal note from her (through her assistant, Jan) congratulating me on my recovery and wishing me success with my book, *Alpha Chick*.

The more entrenched I became in my recovery and spiritual practices, the more I realized that the chaotic journey of my life had a meaningful purpose. I was here to help other women step out of their pain, and discover their power and purpose. By sharing my story, I would help others learn that the past does not define who we are today. Indeed, we have the power to choose a different path—to choose happiness!

The road to happiness was a journey in itself. My happiness showed up in stages, according to what I was ready to receive.

When I was drinking, I thought maybe happiness lay in perfection. If I could make the right amount of money, or get the perfect guy, I'd be happy. I spent so much time transforming myself into what I thought other people wanted that I rarely had time to be the real me. I would dress overly sexy, in short dresses with lots of cleavage, long flowing hair, and amazing makeup. I was a powerful magnet for the type of men who love to use and abuse women. They would show up, wine and dine me, and proclaim their undying love—and then, when they'd had enough, they would leave. After lots of self-examination, I finally realized that perfection only exists in things that don't move, such as a piece of art. Sure as hell, that wasn't me—but the real, imperfect me was far more interesting and lovable than the manufactured one.

At first, slogging through countless meetings and messy emotions, happiness showed up simply as a reprieve from unhappiness. I stopped drinking. I stopped the carnage. I stopped dating jerks. And soon, fewer tears were falling. It was a good start.

The next form of happiness showed up as contentment. I could feel a sincere appreciation for where I had been, and where I was now. I didn't wake up each day with a driving need to find validation from something or someone. I began to fill my head and heart with positive affirmations, and stories of other people who had healed from similar difficulties. I also developed an appreciation for small, simple things, like a beautiful sunrise. I felt grateful to have a home and a car, when others in my meetings had lost both. A hot cup of coffee shared with a friend became a real blessing.

For the first time, my life was a pallet of beautiful colors; I was no longer living in a grey zone.

Finally, happiness came through the door as joy. Joy isn't a state of 24/7 bliss like I once believed (after all, life is life, and there will always be traffic jams, unpleasant people, and struggle) but I have learned to savor the moments where I am truly happy. Joy is looking in the mirror and seeing a well-groomed, put-together woman on her way to meet with and support a fellow woman in recovery. It's helping others uncover their dreams. It's my dog, Hannah, rolling over in one of her many adorable poses to cheer me up.

It was these unexpected moments of appreciation and creativity which led to the creation of my first book. I spent four years writing *Alpha Chick*, and it was published on February 14, 2012. I picked Valentine's Day to share my story because it was a gift of self-love. It was my declaration to the world that I loved me. Every part of me. Every drunken, staggering, falling-down second. Every blackout, dented bumper, and excruciating hangover. These things had brought me to my moment of complete acceptance. I felt so empowered as I pushed the veil of shame aside and stepped through to bare my soul to the Universe, crying, "Here I am world, no longer shackled to the pain of self-loathing! Here I am, living with grace and gratitude! Thank you, God, for my journey, for it has made me the woman I am today!"

This is the most powerful form of happiness for an alcoholic: acceptance. Going with the flow, not needing to be anyone or do anything. Knowing, inside, that I am just enough in God's eyes.

Reflection
Questions

Have you or someone in your life struggled with addiction?

What have you learned from the presence of addiction in your life, and how can you use this knowledge to help yourself and others?

Mal writes that acceptance is the most powerful form of happiness. How can you more gracefully accept yourself and your past experiences?

Today, I Choose My Heart

Tiffany Kane

*T*he conversation in my head goes something like this:

Wow, I'm actually feeling pretty good today. For the first time in what feels like a really long time, I feel both peaceful and hopeful. I finally understand that everything is actually going to be okay!

But what will they think? That I am not sad enough? That I really don't care, or that I'm unfeeling? Maybe it's not okay that I don't feel sad. I guess I could cancel. I don't really have to go; I'm sure I won't be missed. But then, I'm tired of being cooped up in this house. It's time for some human contact. I guess I could just go, say my hellos, sit quietly in a corner, and listen to everyone else's conversations. That way, it won't appear that I am inappropriately happy. If I'm quiet, they don't have to know that it's because I'm feeling peaceful. I'll just make sure I don't smile too much.

All this in preparation to attend an informal gathering with people I love. All this to spend time with people who I know love me.

Yes, life has been brutal these last few months. Yes, my husband passed away very unexpectedly after only four short years of marriage. Yes, I am a suddenly single mom to my precious two-year-old son. Yes, my twelve-year-old nephew passed away a few weeks ago, just seven months after being diagnosed with an aggressive cancer. And yes, my mom is starting her eighth month of chemotherapy. But the truth remains that today, I finally feel peaceful. Today, I finally feel hopeful.

And yet, today I am afraid what people will think if I let peace and hope show.

I have had similar conversations with myself so many times that it's impossible to count them all. The first time I can remember deciding ahead of time to behave in a way that was incongruent with the truth of who I was, I was twelve or thirteen years old. That does not mean it was the first conversation in which I told myself my presence didn't matter—just my first clear memory of it. There was an older girl whom I looked up to and considered an authority on how to make it through Junior High School. She once commented that a very pretty girl, who passed us by in a confident manner, was "conceited." In that moment, I knew I never wanted anyone to think of me as conceited. So I adopted a manner of walking that was sure not to draw attention, and started inserting self-deprecating remarks into my conversations. The problem was, once I started saying those horrible things about myself out loud, it was only a matter of time until I started believing them. Walking without confidence physically confirmed those not-so-valid statements.

Today, though, things are different. For the first time, I am paying attention to the conversation in my head. I am questioning this pattern of thinking that has held me hostage for way too long. When will this insanity end? I am in my forties, for goodness' sake!

I start to wonder how much I have missed as a result of thinking this way. How many times have I canceled plans I was actually looking forward to? How many times have I given in to the fear of others' judgments? How many opportunities for connection have I missed because I was sure my presence didn't matter? How many times have I diminished my contribution to keep secret the truth of who I am and how I feel?

Yes, it has been a difficult year so far, and I have dealt with a tremendous amount of loss in a very short period of time. And while it has been terrible in so many ways, I have come to appreciate all that I have learned about myself through the experience—so much so that it would actually be accurate to say I am grateful.

I close my eyes, and let gratitude fill me.

I am grateful to know the depths of my strength and courage.

I am grateful to know that it's okay to ask for help, and that people do want to help. I just need to tell them what I need.

I am grateful to know that, no matter what happens, I am not defined by the circumstances surrounding me. There is so much more to me than that.

I am grateful to know that, no matter how painful, nothing lasts forever.

I am grateful to have my priorities clear.

I am grateful for the realization that I do not have to do anything I don't want to do—ever. I can, however, choose to do unpleasant things that are necessary to realize a desired outcome.

And then, it hits me like a bolt of lightning. I don't really know what all the other people will be thinking—and I don't really care. Today, I choose not to worry about what judgments others may or may not have about the way I am feeling. Today, I choose to live in congruence with *all* of who I am, and all of how I feel. I no longer choose to allow the judgments of others (real or imagined) to determine how I express myself. I choose to live from my heart and connect with others from the center of my being, without fear.

Vigilant awareness of the constant conversation in my head is the first and most crucial step in my battle to live from my heart and not my head. Only when armed with that awareness can I challenge the limiting beliefs I have become comfortable confirming for myself. It takes a great deal of courage to actively disrupt the patterns of thinking to which I've become accustomed over the years. It is absolutely uncomfortable.

But courage, I've got that. I know from my high school Latin class that the word "courage" comes from the root word *"cor,"* which means "heart." It makes me think about the first time I saw an ultrasound of my son. The most remarkable part of that experience was being able to see his heartbeat. Simply knowing that his heart was beating strongly brought me peace and hope about the pregnancy.

I believe that peace and hope reside in the heart; this is one more way to confirm the value of living from that place. And while I admit that I am not always one hundred percent successful at moving from my heart in every situation, the awareness that I have a choice makes all the difference in the world.

Today, I choose to attend that informal gathering with people I love and who love me. I do not, in fact, simply say my hellos and sit quietly in a corner while being careful not to smile too much. Instead, I engage in lively conversation. I laugh and make jokes.

And the best part is that, as I am leaving, more than one person comments about how great it is that I am able to enjoy myself in these obviously challenging times.

Reflection
Questions

Do you ever "prepare" your behavior prior to social gatherings? Why?

_____

_____

_____

_____

What do you think would happen if you allowed your authentic feelings to shine through no matter what the circumstances?

_____

_____

_____

_____

What have you learned about yourself through tragedy?

_____

_____

_____

_____

Chapter
Two

Happiness is …
Letting Go

The Red Chair Project

Marianne MacKenzie

I am a seeker of truth.

I am the curious one, the Queen of Attention to Detail; an eyes-wide-open kind of gal. The one who notices the sky changing its colors from subtle blues and greys to dramatic, sweeping oranges, pinks and reds. The one who can see a feeling shift and change as it moves through a person. The one who feels the subtle energy flow within a bird when she decides to fly ... and then does. I have come to love these parts of myself, and utilize these gifts often in my work.

So how did I miss all the warning signs?

It was a beautiful September day. I'd just driven thirteen hours home from my family's place in Utah, where I'd spent the last ten days visiting and learning the art of canning sweet Utah peaches. I'd driven instead of flying so I could bring home dozens of jars of the juicy treats for my husband and boys.

After two days in the car, I was eager to reconnect with my best friend, my husband. But the man who met me at the door had a distant gaze. Within minutes, I learned that our marriage of twenty-seven years was over. He wasn't interested in working on it, or talking about it. It was over, and that was that.

It didn't matter that we had never actually separated or had serious issues in our relationship. The words he used to tell me it was over were so clear, and so damaging, that the relationship must already have been dead. And somehow, the Queen of Attention to Detail didn't even get invited to the funeral.

Deep inside me, something imploded. I cracked, and then shattered. In an instant I went from someone who had a plan, confident enough to handle any issue that came her way, to someone who didn't even know how to make the telephone work.

I'm not sure how many minutes or hours it took me to fully realize what was happening, but I soon felt every jagged edge of the splinters that had once been my whole, unbroken self. The implosion had not only shattered my relationship, but a huge part of my identity—who I thought I was, and how I thought my life was supposed to be.

I realized that, after all the personal work I had done, I still had a blind spot. I was running my life around my identity as someone's wife. *His* wife. His thoughts, wants, and needs were so wrapped into my psyche that I didn't know where I ended and he began. We had become a tapestry, woven according to the blueprint I had created for myself in my subconscious mind—but now half the threads had forcefully extracted themselves, leaving a pile of … just me.

Over the next several months, it seemed like every time I turned a corner I would find another fragment of myself. Sometimes, those fragments were dangerously sharp, the shards of old memories. Sometimes they were little piles of broken dreams and desires. Each time I picked up a new piece, I realized more fully that every choice in my life had been made with the certainty of this man being in it. Our family, our future, our traditions, our vacations … My blueprint was well-inked and well-planned.

I was on a downward spiral fueled by anger, resentment, and a deep sadness for the loss of all I had worked so diligently to create over the past twenty-seven years. I was furious with this man for taking it all away, for hurting our beautiful family. I felt totally out of control, a victim of the choices of someone who seemed, in my opinion, to have totally lost his mind.

Somewhere in the depths of it all, I surrendered.

I was more raw and fragile than I thought possible. A strong breeze could have blown me away, like ashes from a cold fireplace.

And then, I met my sons for dinner.

I tried to put on a happy face, but my tears just wouldn't stop flowing. It was more than they could bear. They just wanted the whole thing to go away, and our happy family to come back. I didn't blame them; I wanted that, too.

"Mom, when are you just going to get over it?" my son asked.

In my fragile state, those words were too much. I felt overwhelmed with grief, as though I had totally let my boys down and failed our family. I ran out of the restaurant, barely able to see through my tears.

That night I hit bottom. I lay in my bed, scribbling in my journal. My words were raw, sharp, and full of pain. It was only when I read what my pen had written that I knew it was time to make a choice. "I am so sorry, boys. It is out of my control. I am considering ending my life—the pain is so great! When will it f*cking end?"

Reading those hopeless words in my own handwriting was the wake-up call I needed. Suddenly, my ego, my storyteller, was overcome by my higher self. "I'm not done with what I'm here to do," I wrote. "People are waiting for me to support them, to love them, to guide them to another possibility for living their lives. I haven't even scratched the surface of what I'm here to express to the world. I haven't seen my boys grow into men with families of their own. I still have to experience the epic romance and passionate relationship I dream about, the partnership where I am seen and heard and loved for being me by someone who wants to grow with me. I am not leaving yet!"

How many times before this had I told the Universe to "bring it on?" How many times had I asked to be shown how I could be of greater service? This whole experience, I suddenly realized, was the Universe showing me what I needed to know to become who I needed to be. Some things just have to be experienced to really be known. I now felt the pain many of my clients talked to me about. I now knew the depths of despair and grief. I had danced with shame, and I knew his scent.

It was time to make choices for *me*.

Despite the deep blackness inside myself during that time, I could still open my eyes to witness another stunning sunrise. The sky never let me down, with her orange, pink, and red-gold brilliance. While making my coffee the next morning, I caught a glimpse through the window of the raw, weathered wood of the Adirondack garden chairs

33

where my husband and I would often spend time over a cup of coffee or glass of wine, unwinding or planning our future together. Usually, such a reminder would send me into a fit of tears—but this time, I was going to make a different choice.

I rummaged in the garage and found the boldest, brightest red paint I had. Then, I created a take-back-my-power playlist and grabbed a brush. The sight of me at 9:00 a.m., music blaring, dancing and painting … well, I'm sure the neighbors must have thought I'd lost my mind. I didn't care one bit.

These chairs were the anchor for me to recapture happiness in my life. Each time I saw them, I smiled. I sat in them often, journaling, drinking coffee, or just feeling the sunshine on my face.

That single step toward happiness created a foundation from where I was able to look at my part in the breakdown of my marriage, and the choices that brought me to where I am today. Happiness allowed me the space I needed to move away from being a victim and toward taking responsibility. Happiness created a safe springboard from which I could explore the depths of fear while feeling certain I could come back to a good place in my mind and body.

Time has passed since then, and the red chairs now grace my son's porch. I no longer need them to remind me how to be happy, just like I no longer blame the man who walked out of my life; instead, I thank him for giving me the gift of experiencing an even deeper happiness … and setting me free.

Reflection
Questions

Sometimes the most challenging obstacles are the ones we don't see coming. Have you been blindsided by a major change in your life? How did you react?

_____

_____

_____

_____

Are your plans for the future fixed or adaptable? What do they rely or center upon?

_____

_____

_____

_____

Painting her chairs red helped Marianne create a visual anchor for a new future. What in your immediate environment can you "brighten up" to symbolize a new, more positive outlook?

_____

_____

_____

_____

35

Losing My Sister,
Finding Myself

Christy Whitman

Sixteen years ago, my sister Terrie made the decision to end her life.

Her death forced me to confront a lot of things. In the blink of an eye I was profoundly aware of how fragile life is, how tragically disconnected we as human beings can become from ourselves, and, on the most personal level, how deeply unhappy I was

Prior to Terrie's suicide, I was living what writer and philosopher Henry David Thoreau would describe as "a life of quiet desperation." I was miserable, but lacked the motivation to even try to effect a change. I was nearly $60,000 in debt, worked at a job I hated, and was thirty pounds overweight despite my efforts to get in shape.

My sister's death was a shattering wake-up call. I sensed that unless I created a drastic shift in the way I was living my life, I could easily fall into the same crippling negativity and depression that had had such a strong hold on Terrie. Although I set out with the single intention of healing myself emotionally from the sudden loss of my sister, I ended up learning how to live deliberately as a powerful and conscious creator of my own experience, rather than as a victim of circumstance. Applying this information not only supported me in healing my grief; it radically transformed every aspect of my life.

The first discovery I made is that resistance to any unwanted condition is what prevents us from being able to change that condition. Said another way, we can't become happy by hating our sadness! Whether it's the loss of a loved one, an obstacle in our path toward a particular goal, or a trait within ourselves that we judge or reject, trying to shield ourselves from experiences that cause us pain keeps us locked into that painful reality.

The moment we accept ourselves and our situation exactly as it is, we instantly generate a sense of relief. It may seem ironic, but in order to change the way we feel about something, we first have to accept it exactly the way it is.

Let me clarify that acceptance is not the same as approval. We can accept a situation without necessarily agreeing with it. I will never agree with the choice my sister made, but my own healing required that I accept it. I had to accept that I will never again be able to interact with Terrie as I did when she was in her body. I had to accept that my husband never got to meet or know her, and that my children will never know their aunt or experience what a wonderful person she was. Ultimately, I had to accept that Terrie made her own choice, and that nothing I could possibly do, say, think or feel will bring her back into human form. I don't like it, but I can accept it—and I have.

By recognizing that Terrie's choice was not within my power to change, I made an important first step toward surrender, freedom, and inner peace. My next step was to accept the way I *felt* about Terrie's decision, without judging, minimizing, repressing, or distracting myself from my emotions.

In the beginning, I found it incredibly difficult to connect with my feelings about *anything*, because nearly all of my behaviors were employed for the purpose of suppressing or avoiding those feelings. Like Terrie, I struggled with low self-esteem, and did not feel happy or comfortable in my own skin. Although I never used hard drugs, I was highly addicted to many substances and behaviors that offered an escape from my feelings. I was a smoker for sixteen years. I shopped until my credit cards were so maxed out that I had to take out a loan from my grandfather to pay them. I sought the attention of men who weren't good for me, and even put up with relationships where I was being taken advantage of—all in an attempt to disconnect from what was really going on inside.

I had repressed my emotions for so long that when I was asked, as a part of my emotional and energetic healing, to actually *feel* myself again, I was terrified of what might surface. Yet, at the same time, I was coming to understand that only by having access to our feelings do we gain the power to consciously direct them. In other words, we have to feel where we *are* before we can feel better.

From a spiritual perspective, times of loss and crisis are infinitely more potent than periods of equilibrium and contentment, because the presence of something we do not want brings our awareness sharply into focus as to what we *do* want. Terrie's death forced me to reexamine the direction of my life, and to confront the very real possibility that unless I made some courageous changes, I could very well follow in her fatal footsteps. "If we don't change our direction," one haunting Chinese proverb warns, "we are likely to end up where we're headed."

I had always believed that staying numb to my feelings would keep me safe—but in fact, this behavior was keeping me stuck and playing incredibly small. In the wake of my sister's death, I was called to evolve beyond the self I had known, and redefine what it was that I truly desired. As I allowed myself to fully experience waves of sadness, disappointment, and rage, I became powerfully determined that Terrie's decision was not going to be my decision. I saw that I could use Terrie's suicide as an excuse to keep living a life of mediocrity and discontent—or, I could harness the power of the emotions her actions had invoked in me, and use them to define with greater clarity the woman I wanted to become.

The most fundamental choice that each of us makes is whether we will allow circumstances to dictate our happiness, or whether we will make a commitment to being happy regardless of our circumstance. Any time something is drawn into our experience that opposes the experience we want, we can focus on and complain about all that appears to be falling apart, or we can use that contrast to clarify exactly what we desire to rebuild in its place.

Reflection Questions

Her sister's passing served as a major wake-up call for Christy. When have tragic circumstances triggered a breakthrough for you? What was the result?

_____

_____

_____

_____

Before her healing, many of Christy's issues were the result of suppressing or hiding from her emotions. What don't you want to feel right now? What would happen if you let your feelings come forward?

_____

_____

_____

_____

Often, it's by looking at what we don't want that we can begin to clarify what we do want. What aspects of your current circumstances are calling you to create change in this moment?

_____

_____

_____

_____

Highs and Lows

Lisa Wells

I was at my second Al-Anon meeting, and I was trying not to cry.

It wasn't working. I couldn't get through the whole meeting without breaking down. And I don't mean just shedding a tear— I mean weeping like a teenage girl watching a tragic love story.

This was not like me at all. I was the strong one, the rock, the one with a plan and a great sense of humor to back it up. But when it came to Eddie, I was a big ball of mush.

Eddie is my son, and he is bipolar. While I was sitting in that meeting, he was living under a bridge with no money, no food, and no phone. To say I wasn't handling it well would be a very big understatement.

He had stopped taking his medications when he left the psychiatric hospital a few weeks before. Not equipped to deal with the doctors, the medications, and the therapy, my twenty-year-old son shrugged his shoulders and hitched a ride to the beaches of North Carolina.

"Why is he doing this to me?" I wondered. "Does he know how much he's hurting me?" I pleaded and begged him to stay, but nothing worked. Nothing had worked in a long time.

It all started when Eddie was in first grade. When his teachers had a hard time with him, I responded, "He's a boy. He's supposed to be full of energy!" But soon, the occasional school meetings turned into dreaded daily phone calls. "Mrs. Wells," the secretary would say, "We need you to come and pick up your son." I am sure the school office had me on speed dial.

Finally, I was forced to admit that there was something wrong. I took Eddie to a specialist, who diagnosed him with Attention Deficit Hyperactivity Disorder (ADHD).

I immediately took on the role of protector and advocate. I wasn't one of those parents who marched into a doctor's office and demanded a miracle prescription. Instead, I did my homework. I read books and participated in forums. I made sure I knew my legal rights. I paid out-of-pocket for the best doctors—namely, Dr. Amen, a pioneer in the field of brain scans. I even consulted with well-known psychic Sylvia Brown! When it came to my son, I left no stone unturned; my only goal was to make sure he had a fighting chance.

Those first few years, I was exhausted, but I felt like all my hard work was paying off. Our family started to enjoy a sense of normalcy. Eddie was able to stay in public school and even play sports.

The teen years were a different story. By fourteen, Eddie began to withdraw, and his anxiety started taking over. At sixteen, he had a devastating new diagnosis: cancer. When Eddie was told, he grimaced, and said, "First ADHD, then cancer. What's next, narcolepsy?" Apparently, he thought narcolepsy was far scarier than cancer! I couldn't help but cry and laugh at the same time.

You would think that beating cancer would profoundly affect a person for the better, but it proved to be too much for Eddie. The responsibility of living a life others thought had been miraculously saved for some bigger purpose was extremely hard for him to live up to—especially after seeing other teens in the hospital who did not make it. Over the next few years, he sank deeper into depression and started self-medicating with drugs.

I usually describe life with Eddie as "living inside a tornado." There is a vortex of energy around him, and the entire family dynamic gets swept up into it. Most days, there's chaos and crisis. After a few run-ins with the law, we had to ask him to move out. I thought for sure that would be a wake-up call—but instead, he wound up in rehab, then in a psychiatric hospital after threatening suicide.

While in the hospital, Eddie received the diagnosis we'd been afraid of for a while: bipolar disorder.

I'd heard the statistics. People with mental illness are at greater risk for everything: suicide, drug use, incarceration, homelessness … Terrified of what might be in store for our family, I immediately went to work, trying to get everything under control.

I felt like I was battling on two fronts. Eddie wanted to go his own way, and fought me at every turn. I wanted to reach out for support, but hesitated to share anything about what was happening because the people in my life just didn't understand what it means to have a brain disease. Hearing people minimize his illness by saying things like, "We create our own reality," or having well-meaning friends and family tell us to pray harder, felt inappropriate and hurtful. (I mean, would you tell a person who suffers from seizures that "we create our own reality?")

I couldn't work. I couldn't eat. Day or night, I was always on the brink of breaking down, worrying about Eddie.

That's how I ended up at the Al-Anon meeting. I was spent, tired, stuck, and hopeless. But hearing stories from others who were going through the same thing provided a little of the comfort I had been searching for. Here were parents who loved their children every bit as much as I did, and they were finding the courage to let them go.

The bottom line was that if Eddie wanted to live under a bridge, it was his choice. He was going to live the way he wanted to, in spite of my guilt-parenting or trying to control his life.

Letting go was the hardest thing I've ever had to do. Harder than leaving my youngest son for weeks while Eddie was going through chemotherapy. Harder than having my husband deploy to Afghanistan in the middle of a war. It was H-A-R-D.

Not long after I started attending meetings, Eddie resumed taking his medications, and we began to repair our relationship. It was not easy! It took about three years, and he definitely had some setbacks. One time, after he'd stopped taking his meds for a couple of weeks, we found him living in a filthy, flea-bitten house. He had no shoes, and, for whatever reason, he had shaved off his eyebrows. That was a very bad day. But he managed to pull himself together. Today, he's living in his own apartment and has a great support system.

Gone are the days of arguing and bickering. In fact, our relationship is better than ever—not because Eddie has changed, but because I began working on my own attitude. I let go of the judgment, fear, embarrassment, and guilt—the things that only I could change. And because I worked on me, the dynamic of the relationship couldn't help but be transformed.

I began working on my "state mastery," thinking of my mental state like a giant thermometer, or a gas gauge in a car. The bottom, "empty" place is my low state, in the middle is my middle state, and the top of the meter is my high state. I figured out that when it comes to Eddie, I need to maintain my state at least fifty percent, because if we are both less than half full, nothing good is going to come of that! I maintain my state by taking care of myself first: yoga, massages, meditation and breathing exercises all help me keep my high state. Sometimes, just answering the phone with a smile can change my state—and if not, I'll just fake a smile until I get back to fifty percent!

I am amazed how little changes have made such a big difference in my life. I feel more empowered, and happier than I've ever been. The best part is that, by working on my relationship with Eddie, I've improved my other relationships as well—especially with my husband. After twenty-plus years of marriage, it can be hard for me to be present, and over the years I've often taken him for granted. Not anymore! I maintain my high state with him, too, and he has noticed.

It's been a roller coaster, but I've learned so much from this journey. I know now that Eddie has his own life to live, his own journey, and his own story to tell … and so do I.

Reflection Questions

Is there someone in your life for whose well-being you feel overly responsible?

_____

_____

_____

_____

When crisis points emerge in your life, do you feel the need to try to "fix" the situation? How can you practice letting go?

_____

_____

_____

_____

Lisa describes feeling like she was "fighting on two fronts" with Eddie and others in her life. Where in your life do you feel embattled? Where can you reach out for help in order to feel more supported?

_____

_____

_____

_____

The Art of Letting Go
Linda Bard

*I*t was a Monday, the twenty-fifth of July, six days before my eleventh birthday. The Arizona sun had browned the grass to the point where it crunched underneath my bare feet as I chased my younger brother around our grandparents' backyard. The soulful sounds of The Supremes' new song, "You Can't Hurry Love," squeezed its way out of the tiny speaker of my transistor radio.

Inside, dinner simmered on the stove. The harvest-gold telephone hanging on the kitchen wall rang. And then, my grandmother screamed.

It was the sound a wounded animal makes when all hope of escape is lost. How could a ten-year-old understand such a primal cry? The recognition came not from this life, but of a past life I carried deep in my soul's memory.

Cautiously, I slid open the screen door and slipped into the kitchen. A mixture of fear and curiosity fluttered in my belly. The linoleum was cool beneath my feet.

My grandfather, who long ago had experienced the harsh reality of a Pennsylvania coal mine, sat quietly at the table with his head in his hands, while my grandmother's hollow sobs echoed off the kitchen walls.

Through her cries, I managed to pick out three words. "Joe is gone."

Joe? But Joe was my daddy! My daddy was *gone*?

I wanted to throw up. I wanted to cry. I wanted to run and hide. But I did none of those things. Instead, as my legs began to shake, I hugged the cool, steady refrigerator and refused to let go.

The world moved in slow motion. A wall of pain lowered itself around my heart, and in that darkness, I heard a little voice inside me say, "I will never, *ever* let myself be hurt like this again."

The day my thirty-four-year-old father died of a brain aneurysm in the hallway of our Chicago home, we were two thousand miles apart. I was in Tucson, Arizona with my seven-year-old brother and five-year-old sister. We were supposed to be giving our mom and dad a break by spending summer vacation with our grandparents.

Three weeks earlier, our whole family had driven there from Chicago in a yellow Rambler American station wagon—an incredibly plain-looking "family" automobile. My dad bought it after my mom made him return the other car he'd come home with three months earlier, a 1966 Mustang coupe whose back seat couldn't fit three kids. That turquoise sports car was a lot like my dad: good looking, innovative, and ready for adventure.

The road trip to Grandma and Grandpa's house was our first family vacation. All five of us piled into the Rambler wagon. There was even room in the back seat for a Styrofoam cooler packed with drinks and snacks. Route 66, that classic highway, stretched out before us like a long, black ribbon of adventure—a direct route to places I had only read about in books.

I remember stopping at a gas station outside of Joplin, Missouri. While I was staring out over the rolling landscape, my dad put his hands to either side of my face and slowly turned my head in the opposite direction.

"Look," he whispered in my ear.

There, behind a barbed wire fence, three chestnut horses were quietly grazing.

My dad knew how much I loved these beautiful animals, and wanted to surprise me by showing me my first real, live horse. My excited squeal was almost as big as his delighted smile.

Early pictures of me reveal a joyful spirit totally unafraid to express her outgoing nature and love of the spotlight. I was Daddy's girl with the big brown eyes, the first-born grandchild. The one to make a special twenty-three-year-old man named Joe step happily into his new role as a devoted father.

Ten short years later, on that July day in 1966, I not only lost my dad, I lost my mirror. On the verge of womanhood, I was suddenly adrift. I'd lost the person who had lovingly reflected back to me that I could be celebrated as both smart and beautiful, funny and empathic, innocent and wise.

My father's death left me to experience so many rites of passage on my own. My first plane ride happened in the dead of night during a thunderstorm as the three of us flew back to Chicago with our grandparents. My first funeral was his. My first limousine ride didn't take me to my prom, but to the cemetery.

I remember running my hand over the car's soft black leather seats, looking at the stunned, tear-stained faces of my mother and my siblings, thinking, "This is what it must have been like for Jackie Kennedy and her children."

Then I began to wonder, like a good Catholic girl, whether it was wrong to feel special riding in a limo, while others grieved.

In some ways it was a blessing that I wasn't there when my father died. But *not* being there scarred me in other ways; it created within me a terrible fear of letting go.

For a long time, I carried a deep reluctance to fully experience any joy, for fear that whatever made me happy would disappear into thin air—just like my father. I didn't want to be abandoned again. And so my teenage years were spent searching for deep connection in the shallowest of ways. I felt a reckless pride in how easily I could disconnect from my heart while refusing to commit to any relationship.

I spent many years exploring both my heart and my soul in an effort to heal those wounds. I realized that the wall of grief which descended around my heart that day in my grandmother's kitchen had also imprisoned the happy, unafraid, ten-year-old who was always ready for adventure. But unbelievably, she hadn't abandoned me. Patiently, she continued to reach out over the years, even when I refused to listen.

49

"Linda, I need you to let go of the grief. I'm tired of being held hostage in the dungeon of your mind. It's lonely in here!" she would say, with an emphatic stamp of her little foot. "Happiness is a choice, you know!"

She also said, in the words of my colorful grandmother, "Shit or get off the pot!"

And finally, I did. I trusted myself, and the Universe, enough to let go, and chose to make space for the possibility of something more.

More love. More joy. More happiness.

At twenty-seven, I fell in love with and married an incredibly artistic, adventurous, and soulful man who still treasures me thirty-three years later. Together, we have two beautiful and gifted children. When I passed the milestone of my thirty-fourth birthday, it was with the sober realization that I was going to live longer than my father had. I cried, imagining how my own family would feel if my time here was done.

And then, a week before my daughter's eleventh birthday, I was able to understand the loss of my dad from a different perspective.

Instead of seeing it from a place of lack, I finally saw how rich and full my daughter's own relationship was with her dad after just ten years, and how blessed I was to have had that time with him.

It was a bittersweet moment of recognition. I was now the mirror for my own children, as my father had once been for me. It was my task to help them truly see themselves, so they could shine their lights and share their gifts with the world. It was my job to teach them how to let go, so they could blossom.

Did I hover too much? Did I try to control the Universe to keep them from getting hurt? Did I fall short at times by trying to meet their every need? Sure I did. But while I was trying hard to teach my children all about life, they ended up teaching *me*.

Watching the giddy determination of my one-year-old son as he learned to walk was like having a front row seat to my own tiny Buddha. "Fall down seven times, get up eight," he would have laughingly said if he could talk.

When my five-year-old daughter came running excitedly to me, waving a watercolor painting exploding with the fiery energy of a gigantic smiling sun, I was reminded that joy comes from expressing your gifts.

And as I comforted both my children as they shed their final tears after breaking up with their first loves, I suddenly found that I had become the Buddha. "Some people think it's holding on that makes you strong," I told them. "But sometimes, it's letting go."

My children are grown now, and when they left the nest, I once again experienced the pain of letting go. This time, though, there was joy mingled with my tears. And in those newfound moments of stillness and quiet, the voice of my ten-year-old heart called out again. I decided to call her "Little Linda."

"Now what?" she asked impatiently.

Why was that question so damned annoying and scary?

Little Linda answered, "Maybe because you've spent so much time taking care of all the 'musts' and the 'shoulds' that you don't know what you truly want."

How could that be? I'd been blessed to do so many creative things throughout my life—as a voiceover artist, a racetrack exercise girl, a music talent agent, a model, and an award-winning interpretive writer. That's a pretty amazing and eclectic resume!

But as the Chinese philosopher, Lao Tzu said, "When I let go of what I am, I become what I might be." After listening to my inner voice, and sitting with the fear of stepping beyond my comfort zone, I began to look for a way to discover and realign with my Soul Purpose. When a hand analysis reading revealed that my calling was to be a "Transformational Healer and Inspirational Communicator with a Message for the Masses," it was like discovering a map to the buried treasure of my true self.

Of course! I could help others navigate the blind spots, self-doubt, and uncertainty about what's next. I could guide them on how to listen to their inner voices, and let go of the stories that no longer serve them—and by doing so, show them how happiness can light the darkness and replace the pain.

Some people come into our lives for the "soul purpose" of teaching us how to let go. I see now that the experience of losing my dad was the beginning of my transformation. I love the wise woman I am becoming, but if the time comes to let her go, too, I'm okay with that. There's a joyful ten-year-old girl inside me who is *always* ready for the next adventure.

Reflection Questions

What is your experience with letting go?

Losing a loved one can be like losing a mirror of ourselves. What did your departed loved ones show you about yourself, and how can you continue to see those things now that they're gone?

Drawing on Lao Tzu's wisdom, what part(s) of yourself do you need to let go of to become who you might be?

Chapter
Three

Happiness is ...
Freedom

Of Hooves and Wings

Alexa Linton

Whether I chose horses or horses chose me, I may never know. But I remember feeling the pull, the inexplicable draw, even as an awkward five-year-old, all legs and somber, tentative smiles. The shape of a horse—spine gently curving up to a regal head, proud and powerful, tail trailing like delicate ribbons in the wind—opened my imagination onto rolling grasslands, my sole focus the rumble of hooves in perfect rhythm. When faced with this pure power and riveting beauty, the world and all its troubles fell away.

At age thirteen, amidst a cacophony of horses (in the form of posters, covering every inch of the walls in my bedroom), my first horsey dream came true: riding lessons. As my teenaged friends dropped like fruit flies out of the world of horses, lured by the prospects of boys, clothes, and popularity, I measured my weeks in horse time—in the quiet of the stables, the smells of horse breath and sweat and shavings, and the heat of the softest coat under my hand. My solace was here; the barn offered an escape from a life of criticism and impossibly high expectations (mostly my own), and the taunting of my many inner demons. Daily, I dealt with my own harsh judgments about everything from my grades to my performance in sports and how I looked in the mirror—but not when I was with *them.*

Looking back, I realize I was stuck in a vicious cycle of perfectionism. I pushed myself to achieve impossible feats in school and sports, but I never, ever felt good enough, despite my growing list of accomplishments. I didn't have any tools to process emotion, and the mountains of rage, hatred, and shame that I experienced when I failed to be "perfect" kept growing.

University arrived, and with it, a logistical nightmare. Horses fell to the wayside, replaced by exams, relationships, sports, a poor student's budget, and an almost undetectable depression that coated it all like dust on a window sill. I had become a master avoider, unable to see even a tiny ray of truth about my emotions or my current state of complacency, clinging to the belief that this was how life was meant to feel. Inches beneath the surface, though, I was inconsolably miserable.

When the truth of my unhappiness finally cracked that complacent skin, I was thousands of miles from home, living in a grey and lonely castle on the Bristol Channel in Wales. The first three months of my time there as an activities instructor at a kids' summer camp were full of work, parties, pubs, distraction, and the occasional riding lesson at a nearby stable. Then, suddenly, the summer was over, and the other instructors headed for their respective homes, leaving me alone in the enormous castle.

As I lay prone and unmoving in my uncomfortable bunk, wishing for a human life raft to rescue me from the excruciating pain in my heart, I found myself faced with a terrifying reality. I had to change my life and how I had been living it. I could no longer exist with this constant, thinly veiled discontentment. I could no longer pretend I was all right.

When I arrived home from Wales, I felt like the proverbial fish out of water. The things that had driven my life for two decades ceased to have meaning. No longer did I identify with Alexa the Perfect Athlete, Alexa the Perfect Student, or Alexa the Perfect Daughter. In fact, I had no idea who I was. Consequently, I moved through life like a shell of myself, performing the necessary actions to get by, but dispassionate about all of it. Months went by, and the emptiness in my heart threatened to consume me.

Then, life took a turn, one of those entirely unexpected plot twists that throws the whole story on its ear: I got a car. Now, this might seem like an inconsequential thing, but what it represented was powerful. This car could get me to horses and out of the nightmare of my daily life.

As I had as a teenager, I chose horses. And although I didn't know it at the time, I chose happiness as well.

After four years of relative disconnect from these powerful beings, I walked into the barn for my first lesson with a sense of remembering, and let the familiar sensory symphony flow over me. As I tacked up and swung my leg over, I felt my body for the first time in months, and its joy at being astride. I was home.

That year, my final year of university, was the year I finally dropped a good chunk of my lifelong goodie-two-shoes persona. Up until this point, most of my decisions had been made with the intention of pleasing others, and my primary motivations to achieve were gaining approval and fitting in. But my successes brought me no closer to my desire to fit in and be liked; in fact, they moved me farther away from what I *really* wanted, which was to be happy.

As my awareness of these patterns grew, they naturally started to break down. By my final semester, I'd made enough progress that I decided that my final electives would be courses *I* wanted to take, not what everyone else wanted for me. So instead of Biochemistry and Microbiology (the two courses required to apply for further education in medicine, physiotherapy, or naturopathy), I chose Beginner's Spanish and Philosophy of Religion. A small act of rebellion, but a powerful one: it closed the door on career choices that might have led me to a very different life.

Bombarded with questions about what would come after graduation, I found myself in a state of chaos and indecision—until the answer hit me like a frying pan to the head. In a spontaneous online search, I discovered the British Colombia College of Equine Therapy. Without a second thought, I chose horses.

I applied on the spot (two times, to be exact, and with a follow-up phone call to be sure). From the start, the head instructor and founder of the college, Dave Collins, must have had an inkling of what he was in for with me as a student, but he never let it show. For the next two years, he held my heart and my hand with a gentleness and humility that has been matched by no human teacher since.

59

My gangly five-year-old self, serious and sincere, had a deep wish, a seed of desire that followed her through decades: she wanted, more than anything in the world, to have her own horse. And on a rainy November day over ten years ago, it finally happened.

I met her. My horse, Diva.

We knew each other at once—like best friends who, upon reuniting, feel a connection of love and gratitude that stands the test of time. There was no choice but to choose her. Our stories are inextricably linked. As my dear friend and colleague told me after performing an animal communication reading for me, Diva and I are here to show people the possibilities that exist between best friends inhabiting different bodies. The truth of that statement rolled over me like a wave, and has stayed with me to this day.

From the beginning, Diva was a great teacher. She established herself immediately as my equal, and someone to be respected. With her help and that of my instructor, Dave, my relationship with horses found wings, shifting from one of force, agenda, and expectation to one of ease, wonder, and partnership. My Equine Sport Therapy training, which I originally imagined to be a continuation of my scientific education, revealed itself to be a crash course in energy medicine, emotion, and all things intangible. It was excruciatingly painful and magical all at once, and put me on the fast track to a very different life—one that in my wildest galloping dreams I could never have predicted.

Over the next two years, as my identities and conditioning broke down, I felt myself coming to light. To have been a fly on the wall of my life during that time would have been fascinating, akin to watching a snake shed its skin or a butterfly erupting forcefully from its cocoon. My essence had been there all along, buried deep beneath unhealthy beliefs, paralyzing fear, and rigid thought systems—but now, it was like I was scratching paint off a light bulb; each shift allowed a little more vibrancy to come through. I was a mess, all tears and rage and pain, but at the same time catching fleeting glimpses of beauty and joy. It was as if I was feeling all the feelings I had been avoiding for decades.

Gradually and in perfect time, the tension fell away, leaving me with a life that felt expansive and worth living.

My exact moment of realization is impossible to pinpoint. Revelations came like drops in a bucket; thousands of moments of loving connection with horses, people, and myself. These moments rebuilt my entire foundation and changed how I experienced my life. In reflection, the horses were exactly that: a reflection. Powerful, strong, comfortable in their skin, loving, clear, fierce, resilient, sensitive, inspiring ... They were what I wanted to be. They showed me the way to myself when I had lost any trace of a trail. They were, and still are, my shining beacon in the fog.

My journey to happiness has not been an easy or fast one, but rather one of daily choices and the unwinding hidden in each breath. I've released the countless untruths on which I had based my previous life: that I needed to be perfect to be accepted, that achievement and success would make me happy, that I needed to be "normal" to be loved. Now, I choose daily to connect: to horses, with their spirits shining out for anyone with eyes to see; to my body and its knowing and wisdom; to myself and all the incredibleness that I am; to the deeper truths that lie within. My daily practice might be a headlong gallop with Diva down a country trail, or simply giving her a scratch and an apple, but always, it includes being open to the goodness that my life holds.

As I watch Diva grazing contentedly in the field outside my front door, I know without a doubt that happiness is there if I choose it. All I need to do is get a little quiet and connected, and it will be there, waiting for me at the gate.

Reflection Questions

As a child, Alexa dreamed of being with horses. What were your dearest childhood dreams? How do you honor them as an adult?

_____

_____

_____

_____

Perfectionism is a challenge many women share. Do you consider yourself a "perfectionist?" Does this trait serve you, or hold you back?

_____

_____

_____

_____

What choices have you made or are you making in order to please someone else? What would happen if you made the choice that pleases you?

_____

_____

_____

_____

Falling Apart, Falling Together

Kristi Ling

"Remember that happiness is a way of travel, not a destination."
- Roy M. Goodman

I am so excited to get up every day! Life is truly magical. It hasn't always been this way for me, however. It took a lot of hard work, persistence, and many shifts in perception to get here.

At thirty-one, I was a young public relations executive working in a fairly high-profile job at a big Hollywood studio. I had a fabulous office with a view, a stunning convertible, a closet full of designer fashions, and what seemed like a dream schedule packed full of parties, business meetings, and red carpet events.

From the outside, it must have looked like I had an incredible life, filled with the things we're all conditioned to dream of. Everyone was always telling me how great my life was, and how happy they were for me.

But, you know when you've got a storm going on inside of you, and you're fighting like hell to put a smile on your face and pretend that everything's fine? That's where I was.

I was completely unhappy and unfulfilled, stressed out beyond belief, burnt out, disillusioned, apathetic, and overextended. I was addicted to the approval of others—and at the same time, I refused to believe that I was ever good enough. I had a complete mental block against giving myself credit for anything, and always found reasons why whatever I'd achieved was somehow flawed. Talk about a vicious cycle!

Each morning I'd get up thinking about who I needed to please, and then prepare myself to exist for another day. I looked and felt exhausted just about all the time, but didn't realize it because that

63

had become my standard of living. I covered the bags under my eyes with overpriced makeup. I drank too much coffee—not because I enjoyed it, but because I couldn't make it through the day without a massive dose of caffeine.

It wasn't just the long hours that were getting to me. The corporate atmosphere I was working in was extremely damaging, filled with negative, poisonous people who would manipulate and scheme to get ahead. That kind of behavior just wasn't in my DNA, so I became the weakest dog in the pack—the one who eats last and gets snapped at. I spent my days dodging imaginary bullets, and wishing things were different.

To try to fill the void I was feeling, I loaded my life with lots of stuff. I was always on a quest to find the next *thing* to make me happy. I bought a lot of super-cute stuff that I totally didn't need, most of which ended up stuffed away with the tags still on. My overfilled closet was a reflection of my own emptiness. I took stacks of work home with me, and spent weekends at work-related parties and events, rarely taking a break.

And the worst part? I thought I was doing everything right! That somehow, some way, it would all lead to happiness. But the more I chased the wrong things, the emptier and more stressed out I felt.

A day came that was just like any other. I was rushing to get out the door, but couldn't find my keys in my cavernous, disorganized handbag. As I fished around for them, I was struck by the feeling that this miniscule setback was a sign.

You're done, said my inner voice. *You can't find the keys because you are not meant to go there anymore. Call in sick. Flake out. You've hit a wall, and need to make a drastic change. Do you even know who you are?*

I dismissed the voice, like I'd done so many other times, located the keys, and powered through the day with help from my usual coffee and junk food.

Very late that night, I woke with a jolt, shaking and in a cold sweat. I didn't know what was happening, or how I went from what seemed like a sound sleep into full-on fight-or-flight mode. I sprung up as if the bed was on fire, and forced myself to take a few deep breaths.

My first thought was, *Whoa!* Then, in the next moment, I realized with amazing clarity that my body was trying to speak to me, and so was my spirit.

For the first time, I decided I was willing to listen.

Hitting bottom can be an amazing thing. You crack open. You become unstuck simply because you have no energy left to put into keeping yourself stuck. You become willing to try anything that might help you rise from the ashes, even just a little.

There was a breeze blowing through the bedroom window; I could feel it on my skin. I glanced down at the twisted sheets and the impression left on the mattress by the woman who, moments ago, had been awakened by an internal storm. In that instant, it felt like every part of my world was crumbling—but strangely, there was a peace about it.

Then, something happened. My inner voice spoke up. Loudly.

It told me that *I* was part of the problem. That I had contributed to this damaging, unfulfilling situation by *allowing* it, and that I had to take responsibility, step into my power, and change my priorities. I was on a path to disaster—to sickness, or something worse—and I needed a massive shift in direction.

Firmly but lovingly, the voice told me that I wasn't recognizing my own authority to make better choices and create the authentic, happy life that my heart truly desired. I had the power to change my situation—and, equally as important, my perception.

With a tiny spark of renewed strength, I became determined to stand up and do whatever I could to climb out of the darkness and create the change I needed. To make different choices, unapologetically. To find joy, inner peace, and purpose.

65

I called in sick to work that morning, and spent the day thinking, breathing, and doing my best to pull myself together. For the first time in forever, I was willing to look in the mirror and see myself, and my life, clearly. Although what I was looking at was messy, I could see that it also had the potential to be wonderful.

I left my studio job without anything else on the horizon. It was risky, but *not* leaving was an even bigger risk. Ray Bradbury once said, "Jump and you will find how to unfold your wings as you fall." And that's what I did.

I read dozens of books about transition, health, and happiness. I gave away tons of meaningless stuff that I'd accumulated, and channeled all my newfound energy into growing, taking responsibility, and creating a better life.

One of the first things I found was that I'd been paying way too much attention to what was on the outside: the stuff, the people, the projects, the crazy and unrealistic schedule. I rarely, if ever, checked in with myself to take care of what was going on inside. When my inner voice spoke to me, I squashed it. My spirit was completely neglected.

I began tuning in to the love in my life. I'd been focused on achievement for so long that I couldn't see that all the approval I needed was already in my life, in the form of love from my family, friends, and even myself. I started deliberately focusing on the things that made me feel lighter and more joyful, like books, nature, cooking, and great conversations. Through these, I discovered what some of my true passions were.

Learning to turn inward, *and then act accordingly*, was one of the greatest gifts I have ever received. Once I slowed down and started to apply what I was learning, I began to discover how to purposefully create much more happiness in my life. It was no longer about temporary highs from achievement, approval, or accumulating stuff. It was about simplicity, love, and working to be content with the everyday.

About three months after I left my corporate job, and with my savings about to run out, it became clear to me that starting my own business to serve others was part of my calling. Armed with my background in public relations and my new outlook, I started my own boutique PR and consulting firm, focusing only on uplifting projects and brands.

When you're on the right path, the doors just seem to fly open. Everything just falls together. A few years back, I shifted most of my work into coaching, writing, and speaking. I wake up trusting the Universe every day.

Of course, there have been ups and downs over the years, along with a few life-shifting challenges. I would not have made it through those dark times without the lessons I learned and the courage I gained through past breakthroughs. These days, self-care is at the top of my list, and I make a daily practice of allowing myself to feel the love that surrounds me in my life. Because that's a big part of what happiness actually is: a daily practice, and a foundation that's there to support you through both darkness and light.

We can learn, grow, step forward, and change paths, over and over again. We can choose to deliberately practice happiness every day. I now work to live in a consistent state of love, gratitude, and compassion, and regularly notice all the things that really matter. I take responsibility for my state of mind and for my energy. Living this way, the hard times are a bit easier, the good times are more frequent and more joyful, and life blossoms into everything it's meant to be.

Reflection Questions

In what ways do you seek the approval of others?

_____

_____

_____

_____

Do you approve of yourself? Why or why not?

_____

_____

_____

_____

How are you working toward your own happiness every day?

_____

_____

_____

_____

Two Weeks' Notice

Stacey Hoffer Weckstein

"When you walk to the edge of all the light you have and take that first step into the darkness of the unknown, you must believe that one of two things will happen: There will be something solid for you to stand upon, or, you will be taught how to fly."

- Patrick Overton

*W*hen I started my very last corporate consulting project, I was told by the higher-ups, "This new client is going to make or break your career."

Lucky for me, not only did this client break my career, it *shattered* my corporate career into millions of pieces. I had been earning the big money, climbing the corporate ladder, and was absolutely miserable.

Let me explain.

For almost six years, I had been working in Corporate America. My benefits and salary were incredible. In a time when millions of people, including some of my closest friends, were losing their jobs, I was financially flourishing. I had plenty of money in the bank, took my family on extravagant vacations, and showered my boys with all the toys a kid could ask for.

For years, I thought I was living the American dream.

That was, until I woke up one morning not recognizing the woman in the mirror. I remember thinking, "Who is this imposter, and what has she done with my heart, my soul, and my inner bohemian?"

Until this point, I hadn't acknowledged that my true self, my "inner bohemian," felt stifled in corporate environments. I wanted to wear flowy skirts, tank tops, and flip flops, not my conservative professional wardrobe. I wanted to leave the boardroom and run to

69

the nearest body of water to paint, dance, and meditate under the full moon. I wanted to live in the moment, free from all conventional rules and practices.

I dreamed of starting my own social media company that would bring inspiring female bloggers together to foster deep, real, inspiring online conversations, and ultimately create a better, more connected world for women and their children.

I wanted to change the world—but for eighteen months after that moment in front of my mirror, I convinced myself that this was just my immaturity talking. I was an adult, a mother, and a wife. I had responsibilities. I was the breadwinner, and my family relied on me to provide for them financially. As my heart and soul (and inner bohemian) starved for attention, I convinced myself I was "doing the right thing." In other words, I was doing what I was expected to do.

I'm not quite sure how I survived those final months in my corporate job. I remember feeling totally detached, and numbing myself with food. I knew my false sense of the American dream was really my worst nightmare. I yearned to be free, but could not see a way out. I had convinced myself that I was trapped, a prisoner of the system. Not knowing any better, I had created a lifestyle based on my level of income. If I walked away, how would I support my family?

And then, one day, everything changed.

One Wednesday morning, as the sun streamed through my bedroom window, I felt an intense ache penetrating so deeply through my heart that I thought I was having a heart attack.

It wasn't a heart attack. It was my heart cracking wide open.

I was dreading working on my to-do list. It felt so irrelevant. I wasn't saving babies, lifting people's spirits, or shifting the happiness and consciousness of women around the world. I was wasting my precious time here on Earth doing busy work.

I hated my job.

My inner child wanted to play, my soul wanted to be set free, and I still couldn't see a way out.

I was working from home that day, so after tending to my children's needs and driving them to school, I plopped onto my bed and began reading my e-mail. I found an "urgent" message from that corporate client (the one that was going to make or break my career) telling me to review and edit a two-hundred-page presentation by noon.

"More dreadful busy work," I sighed, and opened the presentation.

I can't remember the exact details of what happened next, but I'm pretty sure I had an anxiety attack. I was gazing at the words and graphics in the document, but I couldn't process the information.

I reminded myself to breathe, quietly closed my computer, crawled under my blanket, and cried.

"I can't do this anymore," I told myself, "I'm done. This is killing me. I cannot do this anymore."

For a year and a half, I'd known that my job was slowly draining the life out of me, and I had just let it happen. That morning, while emotionally and spiritually drained, I finally cried out for help.

"I'm done playing the role of a corporate professional" I shouted. "This is not my calling. I am not being true to myself. I *cannot* do this anymore. I'm done."

In that moment, I realized I had sacrificed the last six years of my life to a job I hated. Instead of standing in my power, I had played the good-girl role, doing what I thought I was "supposed" to do instead of what my heart and soul wanted. I realized just how much I had sacrificed the life I wanted in exchange for a big pay check. Yes, my six figure income had provided a lot for my family— but at what expense? The golden handcuffs were no longer serving me, they were suffocating me.

There had to be a different way.

Then, I heard my inner wisdom whisper. "There is another path. You can choose not to go back to work today. You can choose to *never* go back to work. You are at choice. You can walk into the unknown, and choose another path."

My mind was spinning. "Another path ..." I pondered. Could this really be true? How would I pay my bills?

Then, out of nowhere, I thought "Maybe I could quit my job, live on my savings for three months, and give myself the summer to get my inspiring social media business up and running."

I felt a spark of possibility.

In that moment, I finally let myself believe another path was possible. I had no idea how it would all unfold, yet I made the decision to believe it would all come into form. I was done believing there was no other way to live. I was done fearing the unknown. I was done being miserable eight-plus hours a day, five days a week. And since I was no longer willing to do what I'd been doing, there was no choice but to do something else.

Looking back, I think that decision may have saved my life. It certainly saved my soul.

On that Wednesday morning, I decided to stand in my power, walk into the unknown, and say "Yes!" to life on my own terms. It was time to pierce through the fears that had been weighing me down for far too long. I let them go, and chose happiness over despair.

Making this decision was exhilarating. I felt as if I was standing outside of my body watching my dreams unfold.

And then, while standing in my truth and owning my choices, I picked up the phone and I told my manager I was giving my two weeks' notice.

In that moment, I began to create my happily ever after.

As I hung up the phone, a sensation of relief washed over me. "I'm finally on the other side," I told myself. It was as if I had just crossed the Red Sea into freedom.

Full of excitement, I was ready to plant new seeds, to fully bloom, to prosper in a whole new way. I had set my inner bohemian free, and given myself permission to follow my dreams.

When I left my corporate job, I started on a life-long spiritual journey back to myself. I created the space I needed to rediscover what matters most in my life. I started meditating, using my voice for social good, giggling more with my children, being of service, and being authentically me.

Three months after I left the corporate world, I founded Inspiring Social Media, Inc. and started implementing social media engagement campaigns for some of today's most transformational female entrepreneurs. I was living my dream.

Inspired by my spiritual mentor Christine Arylo, I vowed to never again settle for less than what my heart and soul desire. I now realize that anything is possible, as long I choose self-love over fear, embrace abundance over scarcity, and listen to my inner truth over conventional wisdom.

Reflection Questions

Is your career in alignment with who you are and what you believe in?

_____

_____

_____

_____

Have you ever stayed in a job or situation longer than was healthy? What finally prompted you to create change?

_____

_____

_____

_____

If money and time were of no consequence, what would you want to do with your life?

_____

_____

_____

_____

This Sacred Life

Shann Vander Leek

*T*he phone rang at exactly 11:11 a.m.

11:11 again. Why did that sequence of numbers always seem to be popping up in front of me?

I almost didn't pick up the phone. I was deep into budget planning for my high-powered job in television advertising, and didn't want to interrupt the painstaking process. On the third or fourth ring, however, I answered the call that would forever change the course of my life.

On the line was John, a charismatic former colleague and master negotiator. Without preamble, he offered me a mind-blowing position with a media company in Austin, Texas. The promotion would mean a brag-worthy management position, a virtually unlimited expense account, and a truly insane salary several times greater than the six figures I was already bringing in. Talk about an ego boost and a fork in my road!

Part of me was jumping up and down screaming, "Hell, yes! This is it!" This was my chance to manifest a lifestyle that most people can only dream about. I would be an instant millionaire! But the other part of me was overwhelmed with all of the changes that would come with my new role and lifestyle transformation.

John was certain that I should step up my game, join his company, and get rich quick. But my intuition was telling me to consider his offer with great care.

While I was weighing my options, a friend gave me a photocopy of one of the chapters of the Tao Te Ching. This is the passage that got my attention:

"Fame or integrity: which is more important? Money or happiness: which is more valuable? Success or failure: which is more destructive? If you look to others for fulfillment, you will never truly be fulfilled. If your happiness depends on money, you will never be happy with yourself. Be content with what you have; rejoice in the way things are. When you realize there is nothing lacking, the whole world belongs to you."

Lao Tzu's words struck a deep chord in me. What would it really mean for me to choose fame and fortune, I wondered?

One of the biggest drawbacks to the new position was the need to uproot my family. My husband and I adored living in northern Michigan. In a world where kids grow up far too fast, our little community would give our baby daughter, Marin (who was not quite two at the time) a chance to truly experience her childhood. We felt that schools with small classrooms and an area with small-town values were in her best interest. My husband moved a lot growing up, and felt that he missed out on having a home base with long-time friends. I was quite precocious, and grew up way too fast; I wanted our daughter to be able to be a child for as long as possible in a safe place surrounded by water, woods, and wildlife. Together, we were hell-bent on giving her what we missed out on.

Ultimately, after several conversations and with the understanding that there was nothing lacking in our lives, we chose to stay put. We were happy and comfortable. The financial rewards of a new, high-powered position were not enough to move us away from our family and the pristine landscape we loved.

I chose my family first. I chose happiness over stacks of cash. I chose to rejoice in the way things were. No regrets.

But life didn't go on as usual. That dream job offer and the passage of the Tao had changed everything for me. It was as if the shades had been lifted to brighten up my world. I became inspired to celebrate my life—to rejoice in the way things were.

It was time to let go of choices, roles and behaviors that were no longer serving me, and make more room for more peace, gratitude and joy. I began the journey of spiraling back to the center of who I really am (and have been, all along).

Shortly after making the decision to stay, I realized that I'd kicked my body to the curb for far too long. I was ready to get moving again—but what to do? Friends invited me to a check out a martial arts class, thinking I'd enjoy it, and they were right! I started practicing Kuntaw (Filipino hand and foot fighting), which, after a couple of years, led me to my first Yoga class.

Everything, and I mean *everything,* began to shift at this time in my life. I felt a higher level of consciousness than I'd ever felt before. I was being reborn—birthing myself, in the way I had birthed Marin just two years before. Kuntaw and Yoga became the catalysts for a cataclysmic mind shift. I realized that I was no longer content with my corporate career, and, after a period of deliberate transition, I unlocked my golden handcuffs, embraced my spirituality, and set off down a path of entrepreneurial freedom. I have never looked back.

When I connect the dots today, I can clearly see the chain of events that opened my heart to a new way of being. By choosing my family, I took the first step toward choosing happiness—for them, and for myself. Along the way, I've also learned to embrace my feminine sovereignty and creative expression, both of which have led me to dozens of life-altering experiences. I've taken a liking to photography, written my first book and coauthored four more, sat in silent retreat, become a certified Yoga teacher, journaled my heart out, smudged my face off, embraced my shadow, and participated in several healing sweat lodge ceremonies. About five years ago, I cofounded the wildly popular Anxiety Slayer podcast to help myself and others wipe out the fear and discomfort of anxiety. In late 2012, I created the Transformation Goddess Experience, where women can come for a soulful, sensual, and sacred experience. My Sacred Heart teachings program was born after doing some deep healing work around my once-broken relationship with my father.

So many gifts have been birthed since stepping into my power. The sacred life I've crafted flows with beauty, compassionate self-care, and feminine ritual. My favorite sacred feminine rituals include a daily gratitude practice, joy-spotting, painting, tending my garden, and creating a warm and beautiful home environment. I light candles and burn my favorite incense every day. I honor my natural feminine rhythms and do my best to ebb and flow with the cycles of the moon. I regularly smudge my energetic field and clear the energy in our home. I massage my body with coconut or sesame oil to ground myself, and often soak my bones in a hot bath. Before I chose to follow my heart, I had no time or energy for any of these things. In letting go the pursuit of fame and fortune, I've found something infinitely more important: the ability to love and nurture myself.

I have re-read the Tao Te Ching several times over the years since I turned down John's offer. Lao Tzu's ancient prose was my gateway to discovering my spirituality and my happiness. The quote that changed my mind, and my life, is prominently displayed over my sacred altar to this day.

Choosing to live in a state of gratitude and to be content with the way things are, while remaining vigilant about letting go of the things that no longer serve me, is a healthy (and sometimes challenging) daily practice. By continually stepping up to the challenge, I have become a fierce warrior who is also divinely feminine. A great deal of my strength comes from the courage to be transparent, flexible and vulnerable. With me, what you see is what you get. I'm okay with that, because everything I need is already inside of me. As Lao Tzu wrote: "When you realize there is nothing lacking, the whole world belongs to you."

Reflection Questions

Where in your life do you find that you are relying on external things, like money and success, to bring you happiness?

_____

_____

_____

_____

What would your life be like if you learned to be content with the way things are in the present moment?

_____

_____

_____

_____

How do you define your "sacred life?"

_____

_____

_____

_____

Chapter
Four

Happiness is ...
Forgiveness

Crimson Flowers

Shelley Lundquist

*F*or over thirty years, I could not bear the sight of red flowers. They always came companioned with caustic flashbacks of blood splattered over sun-kissed skin; blood that randomly redecorated my sister's small swimsuit with tiny crimson flowers before spreading beneath her, where she lay almost lifeless on the cracked concrete, as on a drying canvas.

Every re-enactment played out in my mind in merciless slow motion, swiftly disorienting, and invariably leaving me with ears ringing, the pain of a sucker punch to the stomach, and caught in the clutches of a cold sweat. And every time, I would breathe through it, accepting my penance for carelessly crossing the street on a red light and becoming the thirteen-year-old catalyst for the premature death of my little sister.

I desperately wanted my mother's forgiveness, but she was lost in her own pain. So I accepted that I deserved neither absolution nor compassion.

I spent a few years with my suitcase packed, moving between the houses of friends and family, but a change of address never helped. My guilt always traveled with me.

At sixteen, I took to the streets, and found refuge under the cave-like canopy of an old battered bridge. I would hold my breath when anybody passed overhead, making a chameleon effort to disappear into the graffiti while my traitorous heart thumped so loudly it threatened to give me away.

Thankfully, I was not alone for long. I discovered that lost people have their own tribes, and found temporary harbor with a family with none of the baggage of my own. I was shown kindness by people who had not much more than I. A shared sandwich, a cup of warm coffee; everything was sweetened by the generosity of non-judging eyes. Sometimes, when it was raining, I would be granted precious floor space in a corner of a dilapidated building, and would temporarily abandon the bridge for the sanctity of four walls.

I spent most of my days reading at the library, emerging to the protection of Tiny Tom, a burly 6'4" giant with a scruffy black beard and a score of skull tattoos. People said he was dangerous, but his dark eyes would soften when he smiled at me, and I felt safe whenever he was near.

Even though I couldn't see it then, the Universe was always looking out for me.

In time, I did return home—partly to finish school, and partly because my doctor had confirmed that you can, in fact, get pregnant the first time you have sex, even if your friends don't. I returned home without admonition, and was greeted with quiet acquiescence from my mother.

And so, just after I turned seventeen, I welcomed my first child into the world. My son's beautiful blue eyes and the bright orange peach fuzz on his perfect head melted my heart. He was the grace that guided me to want more, at least for his sake.

Still, part of me believed, unequivocally, that I did not deserve to be happy. No matter what signs the Universe sent, I blindly turned away.

So, the Universe sent me something more.

One day, cycling along on the sidewalk on the wrong side of the road, I was so lost in thought that, despite the bells clanging, I did not notice the railway arm descending on the other side. Nor did I detect the roar of the train until, suddenly, it was looming over me. Horror-struck, I realized that there was nothing I could do to escape. I watched, stupefied, as the train sped toward me in slow motion.

And although I don't remember making the choice, for some reason I turned my front tire to the left. As the train struck me head on, I went over on my side, in front of it, and was dragged beneath.

Miraculously, the newly appointed angle of my front tire shifted the position of my bike, causing the back tire to lift, catch the cowcatcher, and safely pin me there. That choice was to save my life,

I felt an all-encompassing sense of calm. Nothing flashed before my eyes. I was not afraid; rather, I was surrounded in warmth and light. I was above myself, beneath myself, within myself. I *was* the light, and I heard the echo of words reminding me that I was here with a purpose.

Despite this miracle, despite my awe, I chose again to turn away. I was still too tightly tied to the illusion of punishment I had created in my mind.

I finished high school and went on to university, where I dabbled with an unremarkable education. My biggest takeaway was the memory of lying bruised and beaten on the floor of the ladies' bathroom on campus, my clothes torn, and the spirals of my russet hair strewn like spreading blood across the tile. Swimming in and out of consciousness, I noticed that my skirt had been randomly redecorated with tiny crimson flowers of my own blood. I wound my sweater tightly around me, a cocoon to cover my shame, as I rose and slowly walked home.

I didn't report the occurrence; I still believed that pain was part of my penance. On I struggled, not knowing that focusing on pain and lack only gets you more pain and lack.

I worked my way through a parade of unhealthy and abusive relationships, including five fiancés, one of whom I only set my sights on simply because he didn't like me when we met. I set out to prove him wrong, perhaps in an effort to prove something to myself—but in the end, as always, I could find no reason to stay, and moved on.

From somewhere deep inside, a message was trying to get through, but I would not yet hear it. I spent a lot of time wishing for someone else to give me the love I needed to give to myself. I had become the sanctimonious scourge of my own destiny, ensuring that I would never find the peace of mind or forgetfulness I desperately sought.

I had my second child just shy of my thirtieth birthday. A girl this time, with gorgeous auburn tresses. Again a single mom, I maneuvered as best I could, but parenting though my own filters was a challenge. I wanted so much for them, more than I had ever dreamed of for myself, and I pushed in moments when I should have been more accepting.

I worked hard, and started my own business as a marketing consultant. Through a referral, I found myself standing before a center for abused women, where I would take on a role in public relations. I had no idea when I arrived that the Universe had lured me there to begin my healing.

And so it began. It was like removing a pair of dark sunglasses that had long held hidden all the exquisite colors of the world around me. I saw suffering, and I wanted to ease it. I saw joy, and I wanted to be a part of it. I found the courage to look past all the blood-painted pictures that garnished the gallery walls of my mind, and ventured forth into a new world of possibility. I discovered the power of gratitude, and gifted many a gratitude journal to those still lost in despair.

I spent seven life-changing years at that center, in the company of many wonderful warrior women. I now counted myself amongst them.

Having learned to pay attention and follow the signs the Universe sent my way, I began to walk my path, and see that those whose paths intersected mine were all aspects of myself, clamoring for love. I saw the light in others, the light that they themselves could not see, and I found great joy in helping them take off their own dark glasses.

At last, with courage, I said farewell to the center and blazed a path in a new direction.

In deciding to become a Timeline therapist, coach, and hypnotherapist at the master and trainer levels, I was required, as part of my board certifications, to undergo breakthroughs of my own. I finally had to face myself. There was no way around it.

During the breakthrough process with my own coach, I came to see and to understand how my limiting beliefs had shaped my life. And during a parts integration technique for internal conflict,

I lovingly brought the part of me that believed I did not deserve to be happy—that scared, thirteen-year-old part of me—back into congruity with the truth of who I am.

I let loose the pain-wracked sobs I'd been holding in for far too long. With my nose running and hot tears pouring down my face, I let it all go.

This was the moment I finally chose happiness. I chose *me*.

Today, the images I thought would stain my soul forever remain gone. When I think of my sister now, it is with echoes of laughter, and memories of us carousing together as children. When I see myself in the mirror, I smile at the person I discovered underneath all the pain—a passionate woman with a huge heart.

Happiness is alive and well within me. By loving, forgiving, and accepting myself and all others, I uncovered my Light—and stepped fully into my role as the designer of my destiny. It is my joy to help others do the same.

Since my choice to let my past go, all my relationships have irrevocably changed. I am a more loving mother, partner, and person. I released my beliefs about how things "should" be, and now live in the present moment, recognizing that my experience will always be derived from whatever energy I choose to bring to it. In opening my heart, it overflows with love and compassion. Daily, I wield my magic, and create my own opus in harmony with the Universe.

Oh, how I laugh when I remember how hard I made my journey! I can honestly say that I'm grateful for all I have endured, because I am now blessed with the awareness that I am so much more than anything that could ever happen to me. I've taken down the gruesome pictures that once hung in the gallery of my mind, and replaced them with a motion picture where I am the heroine of my own life. This is happiness to me: honoring who I am in action.

And, blessedly, where red flowers once seemed so brutally oppressive, I now look at them with a smile of appreciation for their graceful elegance and vibrant beauty.

Reflection
Questions

Do you believe that you deserve to be happy? Why? Why not?

Letting go was a big part of the healing process for Shelley. What events in your past do you need to release in order to choose happiness in the present?

Like Shelley's crimson flowers, mental images and memories play a big part in shaping our vision of ourselves. What images do you carry that serve you? Which cause you fear, or hold you back?

My First Breath

Laura Clark

I took my first real breath when I was thirty-five years old.

It became apparent when I was a teenager that breathing was difficult for me. Overall, I had a pretty idyllic upbringing. I was nurtured, loved, and given many opportunities to learn and be happy. But things shifted in my teenage years, when my father took a job as a teacher at a boarding school.

Faculty children were allowed to attend this school as a benefit to their parents' employment. We were lovingly referred to as "Fac-Brats," and we lived in the in-between: not boarders, not day students. There was no place I fit in, and I became more isolated every day. My living space was actually attached to the boys' dormitory that my dad oversaw.

My mom's demons were also surfacing at this time. She had depression, and because I was in and out of the home all the time between classes, I saw it firsthand. I didn't understand it. When she wasn't committed to an appointment, she would spend hours sleeping or crying on the couch. My teenage eyes saw a quitter. It was so hard on me. I just wanted my mom to be happy. *I* just wanted to be happy.

I noticed that my mom lit up whenever one of her children did something she was proud of, so I strove to make good grades, pushed myself to excel in athletics, and tried to help out around the house. Keeping busy also kept me from having to face the loneliness and isolation in my school life.

And so my cycle of overachieving began. I didn't know what I was working so hard for, or what I wanted to be. I only knew that I didn't want to be like my mom.

I kept myself so busy for so long that I totally failed to notice that depression was creeping into my own life. By my junior year in college, I was taking an overload of classes and working four different jobs. I didn't have many close friends, but I faked a smile in an effort to find some while I worked toward my chosen career in health and wellness. After college, I became an aquatic director at my local YMCA. I was on a stellar career path, and anything but lazy.

Throughout my twenties, I continued to check on my mom, who was still battling depression, daily—but when I was recruited for a job at an out-of-state YMCA, I jumped at the opportunity. "A move will take me away from caring for Mom," I thought. "A move will make me happy." But it did not.

Six months later, my schedule looked like this: get up early for work, put in ten to twelve hours, come home exhausted, sit in front of the TV, grab anything I could to eat (typically ice cream, because it made me feel better). I would zone out, but rarely slept. My life was all work and no pleasure. I was alone, isolated, miserable, and running on autopilot.

One lonely Sunday, curled up on the couch in a ball of tears, I finally admitted to myself that I was suffering from major depression. I could no longer deny it: I was just like my mom.

To my depressed mind, this was the worst thing that could have happened. "You're so lazy," my mind said. "How did you end up here?"

As my depression took over, my work started suffering. My boss suggested I get some help, so I started seeing a counselor. I also started taking anti-depressants and sleeping pills, but they didn't help. My self-esteem was at rock bottom.

One night, sitting on the couch with all my pills lined up in front of me, I found myself sobbing so hard I couldn't catch my breath. Was this cycle of pain going to be mine for the rest of my life? After all, my mom had been battling her own depression for most of her life. "And you're just like her," my treacherous mind said. "Lazy and useless." It would be so very easy to end it all.

I cried so hard, thinking of my own suicide, that I actually forgot to take the pills.

Exhausted by my gut-wrenching sobbing, I finally fell asleep. It wasn't a deep sleep, but rather the kind of sleep where you simply stare into space unable to do anything—when you're not here, but not there either.

In this in-between state, my grandmother came to me. She had always been my "go-to" person when things got tough in high school and college. Now, after her passing, she was standing in front of me, ready to be supportive again.

"Lambie," she said. It was her nickname for all of her granddaughters. Hearing it warmed my heart. "What's wrong?"

In between sobs, I told her. "Grandma, it's too hard! I'm so tired of trying. I don't want to be here. I'm miserable!"

She listened compassionately to my words, and when I was done, she spoke. "Laura," she said firmly. "If you don't want to be miserable, then don't be. It's a choice. Choose something else." And with that, she started to walk away.

Before she left, however, she had one more thing to say to me. "You *are* like your mother, but she is not a quitter, and neither are you. You have a choice."

And with that, she was gone.

"Not a quitter? My mom?" I said to myself, sarcastically. "Of course she is. And I have a choice? Yeah, right." I started to sob again. I had no idea how my grandmother could believe what she had told me.

"How could you be so wrong when you were always so right?" I asked the empty room.

Eventually, I fell into a deep sleep. The next day, I did something I had never done before in my life: I called work to let them know I was taking the day off. I also made an appointment with my counselor.

As I told him about my encounter with my grandmother, I started to sob again. "It's so hard to live this way!" I cried.

"Well, then," my counselor asked. "Are you going to choose to live differently?"

"I can't! That's not how depression works!"

He gave me an odd, sarcastic look. "So you choose *not* to change?"

Damn. There it was: that *choice* thing again.

"Laura," he said. "Let's try this. Let's look at your mom differently."

"No." I was firm in my response. "I've spent too much time looking at her."

"Have you?" he asked. "Or are you still looking at her through petulant teenage eyes?"

"Ouch!" I crossed my arms and huffed. Loudly.

He continued. "Are you willing to choose to see her with compassion? Can you forgive her for having a disease?"

Time ticked by as we sat there, silent. He stared at me, and I stared at the wall. Finally, my eyes welled with tears, and I said, very softly, "Yes, I can. I do. I choose differently." It was an unrecognizable voice; hard to hear, and harder to understand.

"Good. Now, take a deep breath, and let it out. We'll work on the rest later."

That first breath, it was so very shallow. My chest barely moved. It hurt my ribs to inhale, and the breath stuck in my throat. The next was not much easier—but for the first time in thirty-five years, I was breathing. *Really* breathing.

Over the next few weeks, I practiced breathing and forgiving as if my life depended upon it—because it did. As I filled my lungs with fresh air, I filled my life with choice.

I chose not to live with depression. I chose a different path.

I started walking daily. I'd forgotten how much I loved being outdoors, and used nature to fuel my spirit. I also began getting regular massages to connect with my body, and studied a multitude of alternative therapies to see which ones would best fit into my life. I began taking steps into my life based on what I wanted, not on what I "should" do or on some preconceived notion that my fate was depression.

It took time, but eventually, as I began to see myself in a new light, I also started to see all that my mother was instead of all that she was not. It's amazing what a teenager wants to believe, and how those beliefs can become so ingrained. I learned to stop listening to my depression-mind and started listening to my inner wisdom.

In time, I gave up my career to begin anew. I needed space to breathe, and my job with the YMCA could not give that to me; I could not figure out how to minimize my efforts there in order to focus on myself. I registered for massage school, because that practice had been such a large part of my own healing journey, and five years later, I opened my own healing arts practice.

By that point, I was off anti-depressants for good, and on a crusade to keep my vibration high and help others do the same. Depression was no longer an option for me. I chose happiness.

People often ask me, "Laura, how did you overcome such deep depression? How can you be so happy with the challenges that life brings?" I always answer the same way: it was a process of breathing, forgiving and listening. I had to stop everything, and just breathe. I had to forgive my mother for having a disease—and myself for defining her by that disease, because she was so much more than her depression. Most of all, I had to learn to listen to my own inner wisdom.

Today, I breathe. I breathe in the abundance that life offers. My grandmother's spirit was, indeed, correct, and she paved the way for my understanding that happiness is a choice. On days when challenges come my way, I listen to that quiet voice that says, "Yes, I choose differently," for I know now that it is my soul speaking.

Reflection Questions

What belief systems did you develop as a child or teenager that no longer support you in choosing happiness?

_____

_____

_____

_____

Are there places in your life where you feel like you can't breathe? How can you create more space for healing in those places?

_____

_____

_____

_____

If you, or a loved one, suffer from an illness, do you feel that this illness defines who you (or they) are? What would happen if you let go of that definition to see the whole person?

_____

_____

_____

_____

Through the Lens of Love

Debra L. Reble, PhD

*D*ecember 27, 1986:

Dear Mom,

After all these years, I want you to know that I love you. For many years, I've tried to forget you, put the past behind me, and pretend that you never existed. Yet, whenever I think of you, I feel so much pain.

I've realized that for me to heal, love myself, and be happy I need to try to find you or say good-bye. I want to know what happened to you and if you're still alive.

Mom, I've really missed you. I wish you were here to hold, comfort, and just be with me. Painful questions weigh heavy on my heart. Where have you been all these years? How could you leave me? Why didn't you try to find me? Do you still love me?

I forgive you for not being there, for leaving me. I want to see you, to feel you, and to understand your pain and suffering. I know you once loved me, and I've always held that in my heart. Thank you for bringing me into the world. Please find the strength within your heart to reach out to me.

> *Love always,*
> *Debbi*

Rereading the letter I found in my old pink-and-brown polka dot journal, I recalled how, for many years following my mother's disappearance, I pretended that she didn't exist. To me, that was easier than having to confront the excruciating pain of feeling unlovable and unwanted, unhappy and unworthy—easier than trying to answer questions like, "If my own mother left me, how can I or anyone else love me? How can I ever be happy?"

As the letter in my journal proved, I'd been working with the concept of forgiveness for a long time. But nagging feelings of doubt and unworthiness kept coming back to haunt me.

My transformational journey of forgiveness culminated in January 2013, when my brother Jim began researching the genealogy of our family of origin. Although I had conducted a year-long search for my mother while in my late twenties, I never found her and thus never got the closure I desired. During his research, Jim discovered that our mother had applied for a marriage license in Cleveland, Ohio in 1968—two years after she escaped from a mental health facility. Cautiously, we began to hope that we might still find her alive.

To better pursue this new lead, I asked a friend, Michael, and his partner, Dan, a genealogy expert, to assist me in locating my mother's marriage license. Michael went to the Cuyahoga County Courthouse on my behalf since he was familiar with the processes to obtain such documents. When I saw my mother's name on the page, memories flashed before me like a home movie: the summer pool parties she threw for my birthdays, the brown and white spotted cow costume she made me for Halloween, the wedding picture with her in her army dress uniform … And my last memory of her, watching her being placed in an ambulance following a suicide attempt.

Michael ran my mother's birth date, social security number, and last known address through a "people-finder" web site, which projected that she might still be alive. Given her known history of drug abuse and mental illness, I was skeptical, yet my hope was still strong. I remembered feeling drawn to move to Cleveland in 1983, the same place my mother had applied for her marriage license, years after her disappearance. Had I been tracing her energetic footsteps, unaware?

Armed with this new information, Michael and I searched military records, but learned that a fire at the facility where her records were kept had destroyed them. We also learned that her mental health records at the psychiatric institution where she had been a patient had been sealed by the state of Pennsylvania when the facility closed.

Despite these setbacks, we persisted. While Googling alternate spellings of my mother's last names, Michael found a misspelling of my mother's married name—"Skagal" instead of "Skacal"—which led him to a military cemetery at Fort Hood, Colorado. Ultimately, we found a picture of a grave marker on which was written the same first name, middle initial, birth date, enlistment date, and military rank as those of my mother. Further verification through the Social Security Office substantiated each piece of information, and confirmed that the burial site was definitely my mother's. She had died on November 4, 1969.

I felt like a door had been slammed shut. Grief engulfed me. I knew for certain now that I would never see her again. I would never be able to ask her the questions that had haunted me for so many years. But alongside the grief was an overwhelming relief. The reason we hadn't been reunited was because she had been dead all these years, not because she hadn't wanted to see me.

Before I experienced this closure, I carried around feelings of hurt, sadness, and abandonment like an anvil pressing on my heart. Some days, this weight made it difficult to breathe, let alone love myself. The more I saw myself as unlovable, the more I dissociated from myself to numb my pain. This made it difficult to trust my heart, create healthy relationships, and follow my dreams. What if there was something wrong with me?

Since discovering that my mom is no longer living, I've been relieved of that burden of "what if." When I imagine her sitting here next to me, I no longer feel any anger or hurt toward her— only love, and a sense of peace. Through loving and letting her go, I can forgive myself for being a motherless daughter. I no longer feel disappointment in my mother's choices or the limitations of her love, because I have compassion for her traumatic life and the love she never received. Experiencing her in a more positive light has brought me into a state of grace, where I am able to accept what is and forgive what isn't.

Embracing and releasing my vulnerable pain made it possible for me to love myself, allow love in, and feel whole for the first time. The heart-based practice of forgiveness is one that I continue to use every day and in every aspect of my life. I know now that my relationship with my mother served a purpose in my life—and in that knowledge, I am able to finally find closure.

To me, choosing happiness is about experiencing a homecoming to your heart. To be happy, you must wholeheartedly love yourself. Rather than constantly looking backward, regretting what might have been, you can choose to look forward through the lens of love, and discover that not only are you worthy of love, you are love itself.

Reflection
Questions

Where in your life do you have "unfinished business?"

_____

_____

_____

_____

What questions arise for you about this person or situation? How do they help you or hold you back?

_____

_____

_____

_____

How can you forgive those in your life who have hurt you, intentionally or unintentionally? How can you view them through the lens of love?

_____

_____

_____

99

_____

The Compass of Loving-Kindness

Stacey Curnow

As a kid, I was chubby and often bullied. One of my worst experiences happened the day I proudly wore my new wraparound skirt to school. It had appliques of pink pigs against a green background, and a group of boys followed me around all day, oinking and snorting at me like I was a pig.

I never wore that skirt again.

When I became an adult, I thought I'd never have to deal with bullies again. Little did I know that the next bully I encountered would be my own kid.

Two years ago, Griffin (who was in second grade at the time) wrote a note and asked a first-grader if he could read it. When he couldn't, Griffin and his friend laughed at the little boy, called him stupid, and told him that he would have to repeat first grade.

The thought of Griffin standing over a smaller kid and calling him stupid brought me right back to my own schoolyard days. I remember clearly what it felt like to be vulnerable, defenseless, insignificant, and humiliated. When I contemplated how the taunts from my son must have hurt that little boy, the pain was so intense I felt it physically. Shock, betrayal, despair, helplessness, anger, anxiety ... all of them were warring inside me.

When confronted with his hurtful behavior, Griffin expressed sincere remorse. He apologized to the first-grader and invited him to play the next day. The boy accepted, and Griffin promised me that he had learned his lesson. In the two years since the incident, I've never seen any more bullying behavior from him.

Griffin may have quickly put the past behind him, but it wasn't so easy for me to let go and move on. I felt like a fraud and a failure. Here I was, thinking that I was a model of kindness and compassion! How could my own son do something so cruel?

As much as I try not to, I often see Griffin as an extension of myself. He is my only child, and I pin a lot of my hopes and dreams on him. His bullying felt like it was my fault, and when his teacher—with whom I'd enjoyed a friendly relationship all year—responded to the incident by giving Griffin a severe scolding, I felt like she had castigated me as well.

I was suffering, and my negative thoughts made me suffer even more. My mind kept spewing things like, "I'm a failure as a mother. Nothing can make this better. I can't believe this is happening!"

I knew I had a choice to think differently about the situation, and that what I choose to think determines how I feel and how I respond. I needed to reach for my connection with Source Wisdom—what others might call God, Intuition, or Spirit—but at the time, it felt completely unattainable. Source Wisdom was asking me to choose loving thoughts, no matter what, but in a *much* louder voice, my inner critic was telling me I was a big fraud.

Normally, when I'm going through a difficult time, one of my favorite affirmations is, "I know I can figure this out." But, of course, that implies *thinking* over *feeling*, and my inner critic loves nothing more than pointing out the flaws in my thinking. The more I tried to think my way out of my feelings about the situation, the deeper I found myself trapped in the maze of my negative thoughts.

The crisis came to a head at 7:30 a.m., a few days after Griffin's bullying incident. I received an e-mail from his teacher detailing just how unacceptable Griffin's behavior was, and what she thought the long-term consequences of his behavior would be. Except for one line, it was written entirely in bold typeface.

I felt like I was being shouted at. It was horrible. I had no idea how to respond without making myself—and her—more upset.

Worse, the thought of having to see this teacher in an hour when I dropped my son off to school was enough to make me sick with anxiety.

This emotional heavy lifting sent me right back into despair and hopelessness. But then, I heard a whisper from Source Wisdom. With a loving heart as my background, the voice inside me said, wisdom would flow more easily.

I knew then what I needed to do. I reached into my toolkit for the Loving-Kindness meditation.

May I be filled with loving-kindness.
May I be safe.
May I be peaceful and at ease.
May I be happy.

Before I could resolve things with Griffin's teacher, I needed to resolve things within myself. Unless I could love and forgive myself, it would be impossible for me to help my son, or anyone else.

The meditation felt a little awkward at first, and even brought up feelings contrary to loving-kindness—feelings of irritation and anger. But after a while, I noticed that even irritation and anger were an improvement over the helplessness and despair I had been feeling a few moments earlier.

It was a huge relief to be rid of that darkness. Now, I was able to expand my meditation to include others. I pictured Griffin and recited the same phrases. "May he be filled with loving-kindness. May he be safe ..."

Next, I included the little boy who had been bullied, and then, finally, I extended the meditation to Griffin's teacher. I felt calm and centered in my heart, yet connected to everyone.

Best of all, I felt happy and full of love.

An hour later, I sat down with Griffin's teacher. It was a perfectly easeful meeting, positive and solution-focused, and we all felt good afterwards.

The breakthrough had come at last—and with it, a new confidence that I will always be able to find peace and happiness by aligning with Source Wisdom and Love.

I may not be able to *think* myself out of my negative feelings, but with loving-kindness as my compass, I know I can always *feel* my way through, and come out on the other side ready to respond to any situation with a peaceful and open heart.

Reflection Questions

Our childhood fears are often the hardest ones to confront as adults. What old fears have you faced, or are you currently facing? How can you meet them with loving-kindness?

_____

_____

_____

_____

Griffin's actions were a catalyst for Stacey to question her worth as a mother and a human being. Have the actions of a loved one ever triggered deeply negative feelings in you? How did you come out on the other side?

_____

_____

_____

_____

Where in your life can you create positive change by feeling rather than thinking?

_____

_____

_____

Chapter Five

Happiness is ...
Healing

Mending Broken Fences

Mary E. Pritchard, PhD

*T*ears streamed freely down my face as I watched waves crash on the beach.

My husband put his arms around me. "For what it's worth," he said, "I'm sorry this is happening to us."

So was I. We'd been through so much in our twenty-one years together: the loss of both of our fathers and two dogs, six surgeries for my endometriosis, four failed rounds of fertility treatments, the loss of his job thirteen years prior that had placed all our financial burdens squarely on my shoulders. Despite—or maybe because of—all of these things, I knew my marriage was over.

My husband and I had traveled to Portland during Spring Break in a last-ditch effort to save our marriage. We hoped spending some quality time away from our day-to-day stressors might help us mend our failing partnership. It didn't.

I knew this ending was inevitable; our marriage had been on the rocks for years. Yet, until that moment, at some level I hoped we could still make it. At the same time, I knew in my gut that getting a divorce was the only course of action that would allow either one of us a chance at true happiness.

While it's easy to point fingers, the reality was that we weren't meeting each other's needs, and hadn't been for a long time. What made things worse was that, in more than two decades of marriage, I had never been totally honest about my needs and wants—not with my husband, and not with myself. I was the Queen of People Pleasers, you see, and my marriage was no different. Scared of losing my husband if I let my true self shine, I hid behind a façade.

I was The Good Wife, The Academic, The Psychologist, Teacher of the Year, The Boss's Pet, The Wanna-be Mommy. Pick one. I was all of them. None of them were the real me.

I worked full time as a professor so my husband didn't have to. I made sure there were lots of journal articles on my resumé so I looked like a prima donna in the academic world. I spent hours upon hours trying to improve my already-stellar teaching reviews. I catered to every request my boss threw my way. I went through four rounds of fertility treatments, including three rounds of in vitro, in an attempt to give my husband the daughter he so desperately wanted and save our failing marriage—even though I wasn't entirely sure I wanted a child.

I pretended to be happy, and convinced nearly everyone that this was the case. But like all façades, mine eventually began to crumble.

It all came to a head in April, 2013. A month after our ill-fated Spring Break vacation, I had an experience during a meditation that rocked my world.

"You're living the wrong life," I was told. "You need to get back in touch with the Goddess. You will write a book about reconnecting with your Divine Feminine. This book will help you heal and, in turn, help other women heal."

Upon hearing this voice of wisdom echoing in my head, I did what any right-brained, logical academic would do: I ignored it.

Five days later, it happened again.

This time I couldn't ignore it. I sat down and I started writing. Words flowed out of me like water; I couldn't type fast enough. Any time I sat down to work on something besides that book, I couldn't. It was as though time stopped; my world revolved around writing that book.

Three months later, I had completed the first draft of my manuscript. I had also filed for divorce and started looking for a new home.

You see, as my meditation had predicted, as I wrote, I started to change; to heal. I began to realize that I was here for a reason.

I owed it to myself to honor that Divine contract instead of suppressing it to please others. I also began to understand that my life circumstances were my choice, and that I could choose differently. I could choose to live my life my own way, and let go of all my prior expectations about what life was supposed to be like.

I could choose to be happy.

It wasn't an easy road by any means. I call 2013 "the best, worst year of my life." In those twelve months, I got a divorce, moved, and turned forty. I also broke my heel for the second time in a year, which resulted in five and a half months of immobility. By the end of 2013, I had learned a powerful lesson: if you want to be happy, you have to stop fighting the Universe.

That lesson took a little while to sink in. When I broke my heel for the second time, in August, I was told I needed to go back on crutches immediately. As this was the same week that I was moving into my new house, I told my doctor I was simply too busy to go on crutches. A week and a half later, I finally gave in and started using the crutches, but it was with a "bring it on!" mentality. It was me against the Universe, and I was determined to win.

I threw everything I had into proving to the world that I wasn't about to let a divorce, a move, or a broken heel stop me! I launched two new web sites, finished editing my book, started health coaching, blogged like crazy, attended innumerable networking events, and took on just about any project that came my way.

What I wasn't doing, however, was healing, physically or emotionally. I was still fighting the Universe, trying to keep up appearances and please the people around me.

Two and a half months into my second broken heel, my doctor fired me. I had made zero progress; the bone looked exactly the same as when I broke it. She passed me off to a specialist, who immediately put me in a cast, which limited my mobility even further.

I was shocked. How could I not be healing? Shouldn't I be well by now? Shouldn't this be over? I was ready to move on with my life—or so I thought.

Then, the Universe sent me another sign—actually, two of them. (I'm nothing if not a slow learner.) The first one came while I was sitting in the office of a local magazine publisher. A friend of the publisher's, a woman I had never met before, walked in. Upon seeing my crutches, she asked, "Why did you break your heel?"

I responded with gritted teeth, "It's not like I *wanted* to break it!"

Two days later it dawned on me. I broke my heel because the Universe was telling me I needed to slow down. I needed to stop moving so fast and take time to heal my broken foot—and my broken heart.

You would think that, after receiving this insight, I would have made some major changes in my life. Not so much. I was still busy trying to prove to the world that nothing and no one could stop me. I did anything and everything to take my mind off of my heel, my heart, and the reality of my life.

A month later, I had tea with a dear friend. "Do you want to heal?" she asked pointedly.

"Of course," I replied—and proceeded to detail everything I had been doing for the previous three months in an effort to heal.

"When are you going to stop *doing*?" she asked. "When are you going to just *allow* your body to heal and your heart to mend?"

That's when I finally got it. All of that doing, fixing, proving, fighting, and people-pleasing wasn't helping. I needed to just ... *be*.

So I gave up, gave in, surrendered, and watched Fall turn into Winter.

I journaled, painted, watched the snow fall. As I allowed myself to simply and profoundly just *be*, I healed. My foot, my heart, and all the rest of me.

As Winter turned to Spring, I realized that every experience the Universe sent my way was a lesson I needed to learn. I started laughing instead of fighting when life's little hiccups put me off-balance. Instead of meeting unpleasant news with a fierce determination to change things, I started asking questions. Why is this happening for me right now? How can I be with what is happening without needing to change it? How can I be more forgiving and compassionate with myself?

To my pleasant surprise, the answers came almost immediately, and in three parts: the why, the lesson, and the "what-to-do-now." Sometimes I still fall back into fighting and *do*ing, but the Universe doesn't put up with that for long. Pretty soon I get another gentle (or not-so-gentle) reminder of what I'm supposed to be learning about myself. Will I ever be done with these lessons? I doubt it— but I no longer fear them.

Happiness is a choice I make every day. I can look at the glass as half empty, or half full—and I'd rather focus on the half-full part most of the time. Life still happens, but these days I'm more inclined to go with the flow. If events temporarily derail my happiness, I know I am being reminded by the Universe to make different choices that honor my needs.

Several years ago, I started a nightly gratitude journal. Even on days where nothing seems to go right, I can always find plenty of things to be grateful for. I also make it a point to do things each day that make me happy: singing, dancing, spending time in nature, journaling, painting, spending quality time with my man, or talking to my best girlfriend on the phone.

Happiness, to me, is a daily journey of decisions, listening within, honoring, and claiming. Joy is dynamic, not static; it's the heart of authentic living.

$$\mathcal{R}\text{eflection}$$
Questions

When have you acted in a way that you thought would please others, but didn't please you? How did this make you feel?

_____

_____

_____

_____

Mary describes the roles she once felt she had to fit into: The Good Wife, Teacher of the Year, etc. What personas do you take on in your own life? Do these feel authentic to you?

_____

_____

_____

_____

Mary describes happiness as "the heart of authentic living." What aspects of your daily life make you happy?

_____

_____

_____

_____

Green With Joy

Mia Moran

"We are indeed much more than what we eat, but what we eat can nevertheless help us to be much more than what we are."
– Adele Davis

I had it all: three beautiful children, a gorgeous and supportive husband, and a thriving company. It was just as I'd dreamed it would be, except for one thing: me.

I was miserable. On the inside, I had tons of guilt that I preferred work over being with my babies. On the outside, I was eighty-five pounds heavier than I had ever been.

I found myself hiding behind my kids, my husband, or a computer screen as much as possible. Days were organized around the needs of my family and my clients. When I couldn't hide, I found pizza. I would gobble it down alone at pizza parlors all around town, and then venture out in the world to hide some more.

Looking back, it's quite obvious that my entire dream was built from the outside—based on a picture of "happiness" inspired by television, magazines, and distant relatives whose lives I secretly envied—and that I hadn't put much thought into what the inside looked like. At the time, however, I wasn't sure what had gone wrong. I considered myself a thoughtful mom. I bought my kids good wooden toys, funky clothes instead of the typical blue and pink, and the hip gummy snacks from Whole Foods. I sent them to the "good" nursery school. Who was I to be so miserable when I had everything I desired?

This was not my first time struggling, but it was the first time I had to do it with four pairs of loving eyes following my every move. It was also the first time that my Band-Aid of choice—food— did not work.

115

Just to be clear, my eating habits had nothing to do with food. Other than knowing that there were three meals a day, snacks, and sometimes dessert, I had no understanding of what or why one was supposed to eat in the first place. What I did know was that when I felt small, or frightened, or upset, food was there for me.

Food had always been my fix. Too much or too little; it didn't really matter, as long as I was in control of it.

When I was little, I was constantly told I was chubby, and I never felt very well. I regularly visited the doctor for ear infections, allergies, lack of a period, and the mysterious chronic fatigue that ruled my childhood days.

When I was in fifth grade, my mom and I joined a Weight Watchers program. It was the first diet I'd ever been on. All I really remember was eating Wasa toast (which closely resembles cardboard) and feeling hungry all the time. The one and only time I cheated was at a birthday party. Our Weight Watchers guide showed up with her daughter mid-cheat: I had a mouth full of cake. And just like that, body, food, and humiliation were officially connected in my ten-year-old head.

In high school, a friend I looked up to decided to take matters into her own hands. I joined her in eating nothing but lettuce for six months. Very quickly, I started getting complimented on how great I looked, which felt terrific to someone looking for approval. At last, the happiness I sought seemed close! However, the boy whose eye I'd been hoping to catch never did take much notice, and those six months of lettuce were followed by six months of Hostess apple pies.

Happiness had eluded me once again.

And so it went for quite some time. From Atkins, to Jenny Craig, to really any plan that someone gave me, I tried it all. And inevitably, three or four months in, there was the binge: the bagel-and-beer phase in college, huge plates of pasta multiple times a day during my first pregnancy. It was a yo-yo, but at each point of transition, I found a small moment of calm in my busy and critical head. Those moments pulled me forward; they literally kept me alive some days.

So when I found myself in my most depressed moment to date, with four sets of beautiful eyes staring at me, I did what any soul-seeking, hip, *Sex and the City*-inspired mama would do: I pretended like I had no work or personal responsibilities, and went to yoga.

This was no ordinary yoga class. I felt a certain connection to the teacher, and afterward, though it was totally out of character for me, I approached her and introduced myself. A couple of days later, I reached out to her for help—and finally, I was prescribed my final diet.

I was always a people-follower and rule-abider, so I took careful note of everything the yoga teacher told me. She told me to only eat raw vegan foods, go to yoga every day, and buy a book on deliberate creation. It was a tall order, but I was at a point that I couldn't always see how to get myself out of bed in the morning. My mind, body, and soul were suffering, and not even Ben and Jerry could lift me out this time.

What followed was not to be believed. For the next six months, I did not eat one cooked morsel. I lost weight quite quickly while eating abundantly, but there was so much more! My allergies and asthma disappeared. I got my period without a pill. My energy was boundless, and my dentist was shocked by how much my teeth improved. I had moments of clarity where I could see how much good there was in my life and in the world around me, and as time went on, those moments just continued to expand.

By the time I hit the three-month mark, I was getting pretty sick of the ten things I was eating, but I felt a certain love for my green juice and kale that I had never felt for food before. At the same time, my thoughts were shifting away from control and following rules. The food was actually grounding my body, and my soul was trying to soar.

I enrolled in raw food classes to learn more about this new way of living, and started reading everything I could about how food affects our bodies. According to my prior life cycle of diet and binge, it was just about time for me to stop the diet and really indulge. But this time, I didn't feel that urge. I wasn't feeling deprived.

This was no longer a diet: it was a lifestyle. And one day, while on my yoga mat, I realized how happy I was.

The food I was eating was serving and nurturing me. I felt connected to my life, my family, and my work in a way that I never knew was possible—in a way that none of the magazines I'd read could explain. I could very clearly see that every moment in my life, good and bad, had led me right there, to *that* moment, and I was grateful for all of it!

I did have one remaining obstacle, though. For a good six months, I had really focused on myself. My family was happy to see my transformation, and delighted to get their mama and wife back. But in some ways, I had left them behind: this green-guzzling mama was still feeding her little ones mac and cheese, and treating them for ear infections. Two of my children are girls, and I could see I was leading them down that path of "doing what the cool girls do" instead of teaching them to listen to what their bodies are asking for.

And so began a journey of changing things up. I couldn't be all raw, and they couldn't have boxed mac and cheese.

We took small steps together, and today we operate from the inside out. At our family dinner each night, we talk a lot about how we feel, and about how food contributes to that. By eating healthy and consciously, we've become more connected to our bodies and each other.

The cool thing is that I have a base now, a strong foundation that can't be shaken by the next drama that comes along. Somewhere between the yoga teacher's plan, cooking classes, and meditation, I stopped being a follower. I created my own path, and that path has led me to happiness. I have full access to my mind, body, and soul. Even when the path is winding, I can skip along with a big smile.

I now see that happiness is a choice I can make in each moment—and in making that choice, I can inspire those four pair of beautiful eyes to honor their own paths, too.

Reflection Questions

Most of us have a "go-to" behavior when times are tough. For Mia, it was food. What is your go-to, and how does it serve you?

_____

_____

_____

_____

By learning to eat what her body was asking for and trust her intuition, Mia "stopped being a follower." How can you put more trust in your own feelings?

_____

_____

_____

_____

Part of Mia's journey was including her children in her healing process. How can you include your loved ones in your own healing path?

_____

_____

_____

Healing is Happiness

Sangita Patel

My life changed forever on the morning of April 11, 1989.

My brother Niraj and I, along with one of my father's employees, were on our way to pick up Niraj's passport when a huge truck, an eighteen-wheeler, swerved into our lane from the opposite side of the highway and hit us head-on.

There was nothing Niraj could do to avoid it. Our small car was suddenly underneath the truck, its roof sliced off. My brother and my father's employee were both flung out of the car, while I remained stuck in the back seat, my legs crushed under the seat, broken bones sticking up out of my skin.

Covered in blood and broken glass, I was rushed to the nearest hospital, where doctors treated me for head injuries and prepared to chop off my legs. My father didn't come right away; he was busy making funeral arrangement for his employee and Niraj.

When my father was finally able to see me, he had me shifted to a bigger hospital in the city, where they might be able to save my legs. I remained there for the next eight months while surgeons tried to put my legs back together. They reconstructed my left foot and ankle, put a rod in my left leg from foot to knee, and put twenty screws in my right leg.

The doctors did not allow my two-year-old son to visit me during this time, because they thought it would be too traumatic for him to see me scarred and bandaged from waist to toe, hooked up to machines with my shattered legs suspended in the air. I missed him terribly.

My family also waited months to tell me about my brother's passing, fearing that the trauma would be too much for my injured brain and cause me to go into shock and coma. When my father took my hand in the hospital room and said gently, "Sangita, I have something to tell you," I knew something was very, very wrong. But as he spoke, telling me how—and when—Niraj had died, I felt totally disoriented, like I was listening to someone else's story. *What do I feel?* I wondered. *How do I feel, when all there is to feel is pain?* I had no one to talk to. This loss, on top of the physical pain and the loss of my former life, was too much. I shut down.

Once I was healed enough, I was shifted to another hospital, where I started to learn to walk again—haltingly, with a walker and crutches. I felt like a baby, having to learn everything all over again. Once I had the hang of my wheelchair, my family brought me back to the United States.

For the next seventeen years, I underwent surgeries every several months—taking screws out, putting new ones in, taking the rod out, putting a new one in. By 2005, my emotional and physical health were so poor that I could not stand living in my own body anymore. My body became numb. I was not able to walk or even stand without the support of crutches. I climbed stairs sitting backwards, inching up step by step on my buttocks. My muscles were very weak, and so my body ached terribly by the end of the day. I was not able to cook, help my kids with their homework, or do any other normal daily activities.

I saw myself as hopeless and worthless. I felt like I would rather die than go through another surgery. I had finally reached my breaking point. Out of options, I began to pray for a miracle.

Recently, I'd begun reading self-help books by Dr. Wayne Dyer and others, and I had an inkling that there might be another way. There had to be more to my life than pain, suffering, and struggle. So, before the volcano inside me erupted, I turned to the Universe and pleaded, "Help me heal, please!"

The first thing I came across was Learning Strategies. I signed up for their newsletter. The following month, I received an invitation in the mail to their first Four Masters healing retreat. I felt this was God-sent, and I jumped at the opportunity.

As soon as I entered the hotel lobby in Minnesota, I saw all four Masters standing by the elevators! I'm not sure what came over me, but I shouted one Master's name out loud.

"Master Lin!"

He turned around, startled, then came toward me and enveloped me in a huge, warm hug. I felt like I'd come home.

This was just the beginning of my healing journey. All of a sudden, I started to meet my mentors and gurus. Through them, I learned various healing tools like Spring Forest Qigong, Emotional Freedom Technique (EFT), Chakra healing, and how to connect with angels and seraphs.

Each of these tools gave me a piece of healing that I desperately needed. Qigong helped me ground myself and learn to breathe again. EFT helped me to release all of my stuffed up emotions—not just from my accident, but from my entire life. All the anger, frustration, sadness, fear, anxiety, overwhelm, and depression I had hidden for so long finally came out, and I cried for three months just releasing it all. Chakra Healing helped me open up my closed chakras, and the toning/chanting practices brought me harmony. I learned how to invite my angels to guide and support me every day.

Inside and out, I started to heal. I found that I was able to stand for longer periods of time without support. As my awareness of which holistic technique to use for each situation grew, I got better even faster. I started doing daily practices. Drawing on a multitude of holistic techniques, I learned to manage my pain. I began to thank my body for what it could, and did, do for me—rather than despising it for what it couldn't.

Even in my dreams, everything changed. As my internal vibration rose, I started to feel more confident, inspired, and excited about my life. I was even able to experience joy, in a way I hadn't ever felt—even before the accident.

It was at this point that I realized that happiness is a journey, not a destination. I can choose to live this happiness journey with every breath I take.

I remember the first time I gave a ninety-minute workshop. I was asking myself so many fearful questions. How would it go? How would I present the material? How would my physical body feel? But before I could get too nervous, I connected with my heart, did some Qigong, and let my body relax. Even though I was still nervous, I was able to feel joy in my accomplishment. That was another step forward on my happiness journey: the realization that I can use my healing techniques to help myself feel my best in any situation.

I've also been able to help my friends, family, and clients heal by listening to their pain, then tuning in and guiding them toward solutions. On one recent trip, I was talking to the front desk clerk at my hotel when, suddenly, she started to cry. When I asked her why, she told me that she was pregnant, and the doctors had found a cyst on her baby's brain. Nothing could be done, she was told. It was the worst kind of news an expectant mother could hear.

I asked her if she was willing to try Qigong, which had helped me so much with my own healing. She said yes, and I showed her some slow movement exercises and breathing techniques, and gave her some affirmations. She practiced these faithfully every day—and six weeks later, when she went back to the clinic for a checkup, the doctors could not find her baby's cyst anywhere. It was completely gone and the baby appeared perfectly healthy.

That incident inspired me to explore more deeply why I am here on this planet. "What is it that God wants me to do?" I asked myself. After receiving the intelligence of my inner self, and guidance from the Universe and my angels, I learned that I am here to help others heal—and that in order to do that, I had to first heal myself.

We do not have to suffer emotionally or physically. When we turn our focus inward, we can heal anything. All it takes is being open and willing, committed and responsible. The Universe is always ready to help us, as long as we are ready to help ourselves— and when we choose healing, we choose happiness.

Reflection Questions

What does healing mean to you?

_____

_____

_____

_____

What, to you, is the correlation between health, healing, and happiness?

_____

_____

_____

_____

What can you do right now to improve your health and make more space for joy?

_____

_____

_____

_____

Chapter
Six

Happiness is ...
Connection

The Tugs of My Heart
Sandi Gordon

*T*he machine gun the Soldier was wearing at the airport yesterday brought it all back. I didn't actually see the gun; it was in a large case slung over his shoulder. But I knew what it was, and the memories flooded back to me.

November 4, 2009. I started the day at my new doctor's office, getting diagnosed with H1N1 flu. Relieved to know what was wrong with me and that it would just take a little time to feel well again, I picked up the medication my doctor prescribed for me and went home to bed.

An hour later, I awoke with a feeling of dread. I picked up my phone to discover that the ringer was off. I quickly looked to see if I'd missed calls—and sure enough, my husband's name popped up. I listened to his message, and life changed forever.

We'd recently moved to Texas from the Midwest. My husband had a new job as a clinical psychologist with the Department of Defense, working with Soldiers on an Army post to overcome hurts from their pasts while dealing with the sometimes-harsh realities of the present. I was finishing up a business degree and continuing my coaching practice. But my educational pursuits just weren't enough: while my degree was a worthwhile goal, I felt lonely and in need of more significance in my life.

My parents taught me by example that serving was what one did to find meaning. My dad and mom were always doing things to help others—from buying groceries for families in need, to holding the hand of a lonely senior. I learned to give, but I always kept a bit of distance between my giving and my emotions. I was afraid of getting too involved, and of taking on the pain of those I was helping. It was safer to write a check, or donate to Goodwill.

129

But something about an opportunity at Fort Hood tugged at my heart. I wasn't quite sure why, but I knew I had to do it. Fort Hood is the largest U.S. Army post in the world, with approximately 41,000 active duty Soldiers stationed there, and over 20,000 military-family children attending school on the post and in the surrounding communities.

Volunteering with an after-school program in an elementary school was more than a material donation; it was giving my time and my heart. I taught simple lessons, played games, sang, and most importantly, I listened to the children. As they got to know and trust me, they shared lots of typical things like, "My mom has to work a lot. We don't get to play many games." "I love to dance!" "I like singing!" "I like making things." "Will you be here next time?" And some things they shared were not so typical: "I have to move again." (A first-grader.) "I miss my mom. She is far away taking care of Soldiers." (A third-grader.) "My daddy is deployed, and I want him to come home!" (A kindergartner.) These kids just melted me, and I couldn't keep my emotions or my heart even a little bit distant.

That was one reason why my husband's voicemail that day in early November engulfed me in a sense of panic totally unknown to me before.

"I'm okay," he said tersely. "There are active shooters here. They've locked down the post. We are sheltering in place with the doors locked."

Frantic, I called him back, but there was no answer. I called again. Still no answer.

Turning on the TV provided a lot of information, only some of it on point. "Fort Hood has confirmed that the Army post is on lock-down. No one can enter or leave post. There are two active shooters, with many casualties. The Commanding General will hold a press conference in a few hours."

This wasn't the news I needed! What I really wanted to know was, "Is my husband safe? Are my friends safe? Who is hurt? What about the children? What can I do to help?"

Those kids, "my" kids, were locked down in their school and day care center. I knew they were terrified. Did they feel like I did, alone and helpless? Moms and dads could not get to their children, no matter how desperately worried they were for their safety. Kids in the community schools had no idea if their parents were safe, or when they'd be allowed to go home.

I tried to call my husband again. No answer. I was frozen with fear. My mom called. My friends called. My husband's family called. I had no answers for them. I knew many of them were praying

The phone rang again. It was him! I sobbed with relief—but it was short-lived. My husband and his work team were safe for the moment, but the shooter—or shooters—were still at large. I immediately thought about the fact that an AK-47 will shoot straight through a locked door, so being inside a "secured" building was just an illusion of safety.

"What about the children?" I shouted to my empty living room? I paced. Imagined myself as a widow, without the love of my life. We'd been married for ten years and four months to the day. I wasn't done being married to him!

More speculation on the television. I watched, sickly fascinated by the very authoritative "perhaps" and "maybes" as the pundits prattled on and on. I bargained with God: "I'll do anything at all, give up everything, work harder, work less, just please keep him safe!"

Finally, it was announced. The shooter was in custody! My precious sweetheart was safe! And then came the reports: thirteen people dead, and over thirty injured, many seriously. My heart sank for the families who would hurt forever for their lost and wounded loved ones, and for the loss of innocence. This was an Army post! It was supposed to be a safe place!

Down and down my emotions spiraled. With each breath, I felt more and more helpless and out of control, until I couldn't take it any longer. I couldn't wallow in the fear even one more minute.

Although it took me months to really reflect on the experience, I realized at that moment that I had been living my life in fear for a long time before this tragic incident. But after that day (and a previous fifty-plus years of listening to my own self-talk in my head), I'm pretty sure I've figured out what holds us back from living life on purpose. It's not money. It's not a lack of time. It's not that someone else is stopping us. It's not even a lack of love. All of these things may contribute to our feeling stuck, but our biggest hurdle? It's *fear.* Fear of messing up. Of making a wrong decision. Of being judged by others. Of feeling someone else's pain. I realized that day that we have a choice: to live in fear's paralysis, or to take action with love.

I chose happiness that day by getting *more* involved, even though I knew that the pain of those I helped would hurt my heart. I made calming telephone calls as soon as I could get through on the overloaded cellular networks. I posted uplifting comments on Facebook and Twitter. I planned out how I could best serve those who were impacted, including the children, as soon as I could get back on post.

And what I felt was love, empathy, and connection. Not fear.

Living in love instead of fear takes work for me. Even now, years later, I still feel the impact of that day. Every time I pass through the entrance gates to Fort Hood, I check the security level. Has it moved from Alpha up to Bravo? If so, I immediately think, "What new threat has been received?" Every weapon I see—like the machine gun at the airport yesterday—reminds me of our vulnerability to attack, even in places we consider "safe." I must consciously, and continuously, decide to let these thoughts go.

Living in love has meant amazing growth for me. I am ever more mindful of how precious each moment of life is. My heart is bigger, more open. My husband and I are closer and more committed to each other than ever. Through serving, both on-post and off, I have connected with hundreds of people I didn't know before. I've also re-kindled my big dream of having my own business, where I live my mission every day: to inspire people to lead with passion, live with purpose, and contribute to a better world.

I choose happiness in each moment by remembering what is truly meaningful to me. I've found it's not the material things—the new car, the bigger house, the travel, the job title, or the stuff. Nor is it the everyday stressors I face, like bad traffic, my too-long to-do list, or a stack of bills to pay. What brings meaning to life is my relationships with the ones I love and all those around me; it's found in listening to the tugs of my heart.

What does "service" mean to you?

Do you hold back from giving for fear of getting hurt? What do you think would happen if you allowed yourself to give regardless of your fear?

What work do you feel gives your life meaning? How do you express that through your work in the world?

Threads of Happiness

Lynda Monk

*T*hread One

Something was missing.

I felt like Paul had abandoned me and our marriage, even while we were still together. I wanted him to touch, hold, and comfort me in the despair and sadness caused by our unsuccessful attempts to conceive a baby; instead, he withdrew.

I wanted him to come to my grandmother's funeral, and to the hospital the next day to stand by my side as I watched my mother being wheeled in for her mastectomy. Instead, he chose to work, and I went alone. I wanted him to come to Switzerland with me for a dear friend's wedding, but our airfares were a gift, and he didn't want to accept "charity." And so, again, I went alone.

I wanted him to understand the impact my work as a medical social worker was having on me—how regular exposure to death and dying was creating within me a growing sense of urgency to live more fully. I wanted to experience my own vitality through touch, sexuality, and connection with Paul. Instead, I often found myself going to bed alone while he watched television late into the night.

It was not a happy time. Each time Paul failed to meet my needs and wants, I felt abandoned, over and over again. While this might sound like I am blaming Paul, it is not intended this way, especially since it was me who eventually left our marriage.

On September 8, 1998, while Paul drove Luke, our eight-year-old foster son, to the group home where he would now have to live, I packed my car and drove away from the home and the man I loved. My heart was broken. I felt utterly lost.

135

I never saw Luke again. Emotionally numb, I searched for some part of Paul, some part of myself for days, then weeks, and then months after our marriage fell apart. During this time, I wrote in my journal, trying to heal, looking for answers, searching for happiness.

Thread Two

I was placed for adoption when I was five days old, and adopted when I was five months old.

I decided to try to search for my birth mother when I was twenty-one. I craved a deeper sense of substance in my life, a thread of something connected to something else. Who was I, really? Where did I come from?

Due to the vast numbers of people who were also applying to find their birth relatives through the Adoption Registry at the time, my search application was put on a wait list. Years passed, and eventually, I let my desire to find my biological roots fade into the background of my life.

In the aftermath of my divorce, however, I noticed that I was writing more and more about my desire to find my birth mother. I craved answers to the question of why I was abandoned and given up for adoption, and started to wonder if being adopted might have impacted my feelings of being abandoned in my marriage. How might this early life experience of being relinquished as a baby be shaping the ways I needed to be loved as an adult?

A year after Paul and I separated, I received a phone call from the Adoption Registry in Ontario. The application I had submitted nine years ago was finally being reviewed.

The social worker asked if I still wanted them to try to find my biological mother.

I didn't hesitate. "Yes, please!"

Thread Three

The first time I met my birth mother, Diane, I was thirty years old. By the time she arrived, I had already changed outfits four times. (What *does* a person wear when meeting their birth mother for the first time?)

The doorbell rang. The dog barked. I stepped outside onto the front porch, closing the door behind me. Diane immediately took me into her arms and said, "I love you."

She was crying. I started to cry, too. We cried together, and we hugged. We separated, looked at one another, and then hugged some more.

Diane cupped my ears in both of her hands, and traced the edges of them with her fingertips, sending shivers through my body. She took my hands in hers and started counting my fingers as if I were a newborn baby. Years of longing were flowing through us in these first moments of touch.

Standing on the front porch with this woman who was essentially a stranger, I felt her love wash over me like something familiar, wanted and forgotten all at once.

I did not say anything: all my words, feelings, and thoughts were stuck in my throat like thick fudge. I couldn't swallow, couldn't speak, almost couldn't breathe in the presence of her words, as she whispered them again. "I love you."

She looked deep into my eyes. I noticed her eyes were the same blue as mine.

Instinctively, I replied, "I love you, too."

Thread Four

I once read that "adoption is the only trauma where we expect the victims to be grateful."

I was always grateful—grateful that I was born, grateful for my amazing parents who adopted me, grateful that I wasn't left to be an orphan, grateful for this and that. I still keep a gratitude journal as a way of creating happiness in my life.

That said, it wasn't until I met my birth mother—until I felt her touching my skin, holding me in her arms, and whispering words of love in my ears—that I came into profound contact with feelings *beyond* gratitude. I realized that I also felt anger, grief, frustration, loneliness, sadness, and deep feelings of abandonment. At the same time, I felt the power of love all around me: Love from my parents, my birth mother, my family and friends; love that has always been there, shaping who I am and who I am becoming.

Love shapes happiness into many forms. Ironically, when I allowed myself to acknowledge and feel all of these other "negative" emotions, I began to experience a new happiness in my life—a happiness grounded in a different kind of gratitude, one that could embrace both the joys in my life and the painful losses, too. I began to look back through the years and wonder if what had been missing in my marriage to Paul had, in part, been something missing in me.

On the pages of my journal, I wrote into the heart of my experiences, and discovered something central to my happiness. I realized the only person that can really ever abandon me is *me.* Since finding Diane, and throughout the years that have followed, I have learned to choose happiness and unconditional love in all of my relationships, including my relationship with myself. Self-love teaches us that happiness is our birthright, and that we are worthy because we exist. As Mark Nepo wrote, "Unconditional love is not the hole in us that receives the dirt, but the sun within that never stops shining."

Thread Five

Happiness is about being in the present versus looking back. I have learned that happiness is not dependent on my circumstances, or where I come from, or where I'm going. Rather, it exists in direct proportion to my ability to be fully present to what is right now.

The other night, I tucked my sons into bed, snuggled them up, gave them kisses, and whispered "I love you" in their ears. I traced their faces with my fingertips, and tickled their arms to help them fall asleep.

Later, in the dark, my husband Peter rubbed my back, and with his hands against my skin said "I love you." I felt touched by happiness inside and out.

The next morning, I woke up early to write in my journal. Writing is how I make connections with myself and others, and happiness is ultimately born in these connections. Word by word, I also grow in my connection to something larger than myself: to Spirit, to Source energy. My writing weaves the threads of my life into wholeness and happiness; it shows me that the Universe always provides me with exactly what I need. All I have to do is listen, and trust—thread by thread, word by word, moment by moment.

Reflection
Questions

Abandonment was a quiet theme in Lynda's life before meeting her birth mother. Have you ever felt abandoned? How did this influence your feelings, choices and relationships?

_____

_____

_____

_____

One of Lynda's key realizations was that no one could abandon her except herself. How can you be more present to, and for, yourself?

_____

_____

_____

_____

Three powerful words run through the threads of Lynda's story: "I love you." Do you hear and say these words often enough in your daily life? What power and energy do they hold for you?

_____

_____

_____

_____

The Magick of Happiness

Lisa Marie Rosati

When I look back on my life, I must admit that, for a long time, I was not a very happy person.

Sure, I had moments of happiness, and pockets of time when I felt happy, but I never seemed to be able to hold onto it for very long. The feeling of happiness was fleeting, and that was enormously discouraging.

When I couldn't figure out how to get, and stay, happy, I would blame others. I remember one time in particular when, after watching a romantic comedy, I spent hours upon hours wondering why no man had ever done a crazy romantic thing like hijack a scooter then chase me in a taxi cab down a New York City street to win me back after I dumped him. I remember thinking, "Huh. I can't even get my guy to apologize for upsetting me, much less compel him to commandeer a cab and chase me down the street in order to grovel!"

(Now, I encourage you to let your imagination go wild. Picture me giving the disgusted, "I can't stand you" squint-eye to my man for days. Because that's exactly what I did.)

Was I emotionally broken or depressed? I wondered. Was happiness simply not in the cards for me? Was I cursed? These were the questions that looped around my mind. To call it maddening would be an understatement: it was downright abusive. And I was doing it to myself!

I started asking myself, "What is happy? *Where* is happy? Is it a destination? A feeling?"

Now I know for sure that "happy" is not a place that you arrive at and exhale and say, "Phew! Now all my work is done. I've arrived in Happyland, and the rest of my life is going to be Happy!" Happiness is actually an inside job, and you're never done doing it.

Being happy is an empowered choice I must make every day of my life.

As I mentioned earlier, I was often the embodiment of Unhappy. When I look back introspectively at those times, I realize that I was in a state of resistance to whatever was happening in my life. I didn't want to accept what was going on inside, so I looked outside for a way to make things better. I depended on intimate relationships to complete me, and on friends and acquaintances for entertainment. My self-esteem floated on incoming compliments, and I absolutely *never* wanted to spend a minute alone with my own thoughts, lest they erode whatever happiness I possessed at the moment. I was paddling my canoe upstream and against the current, and I was exhausted, frustrated, and, quite frankly, pissed off.

And then, I rediscovered magick, and the foundational sacred practices that finally helped me get out of my own way.

Magick, to me, is the art of creating my own reality exactly as I wish to live it, in accordance with the Laws of the Universe and Nature, and in sacred partnership with the Divine. It's the return to who I am at my core—and, like happiness, it's an inside job.

I've never subscribed to an organized religion, mainly because most religions dictate that their God is the one and only God. It's my opinion that dogmatic thinking separates people, and that all paths eventually lead to one. In my heart, God is everything that is, that ever has been, and that ever will be. God is not a gender. God resides within you and me, and in every living creature. Who you pray to is your own business!

I've been a Magickal practitioner my entire adult life. I was a magical child, too, but life doled out its share of lumps and bumps, and somewhere along the way, I got distracted and forgot my magick (and my divinity, too). In my twenties, I lamented the fact that I could never seem to find my Prince Charming or get my finances in order. I was scared and insecure, disempowered and disconnected, living paycheck to paycheck and crappy relationship to crappy relationship. I had absolutely no faith in myself or in something bigger than myself.

I realize now that that lack of faith is precisely why I felt so damned unhappy most of the time.

And then, one Saturday night in 1995, sitting under the moon at the burgundy-stained picnic table in my parents' backyard, I made a wish. Actually, it was more of a declaration to the Universe—a magick spell.

I'd just gotten back from another humdrum date with some guy whose name I was already forgetting. My six-year-old daughter Chelsea was slumbering inside the house, and I felt compelled to take a few minutes to sit outside and ponder just exactly why I kept saying yes to dates I had no interest in going on.

As I looked up at the stars, I realized that I continually made the choice to spend time with people in whom I had very little interest, just to avoid spending a Saturday night alone, or at home with my daughter and parents.

That truth hit me like a ton of bricks. (I must admit, it still stings a little, even now!) I was avoiding the most important relationships in my life, and for what? Distraction?

Tears flowed from my eyes. I couldn't stop them. Then, my fists went in the air, and I proclaimed to the heavens, "No more!"

And just like that, I was transformed.

Relief washed over me, cleansing away the grime of avoidance, self-pity, and finger pointing that had collected on my rose-colored glasses. I would no longer give my time away. From now on, I was going to be discerning about everything, from the inside out.

That was my first taste of alchemy. In that moment, I was transformed from a victim of my own life to a Creatrix. The resplendent feeling of empowerment shot through me like lightning. I felt lit up from the inside out, in complete control of all of my thoughts, actions, and beliefs.

Oh, yes! *This* was how I was going to roll!

143

I began reading self-help books and listening to lectures by renowned spiritual teachers. I consumed information like my life depended on it, breathing it in and integrating the teachings into my being. I began following the cycles of nature, creating altars, collecting gemstones and crystals, casting spells, and consciously designing my life.

As I evolved, my world transformed. Sure, I had some unexpected crap pop up—but instead of the usual blaming, shaming, and "poor me"-ing, I noticed that I was handling everything with more grace. Eventually the Divine led me to my soul work of empowering spiritual women to magically create an abundant life they love. In doing this work I have found, and kept, the once-elusive feeling called happiness.

Of course, there are still moments of unhappiness or discontent in my life. But instead of freaking out that I've left Happyland yet again, I go to my altar, smudge myself and my space, call the Four Directions, and summon the Divine. As I enter into the realm of magick, I turn my body and call to the corners, arms outstretched, root chakra engaged to Earth Mother, crown chakra receptive, heart chakra open, wand pointed. I light a candle and pray for the highest good for all involved ... and then I leave it all in the hands of the Divine, and listen for the guidance.

Faith has taught me that every struggle I encounter and crappy day I endure is happening for a reason bigger than I can understand. Even though life is never going to be perfect, it is perfectly as it should be in every moment.

I wish for you so many wonderful things, Reader. May your cup runneth over with abundance, health, joy, prosperity—and, most of all, happiness. May you always have faith that today is exactly as it should be, and that you are powerful beyond measure.

And so it is.

Reflection Questions

Distraction was a coping mechanism for Lisa prior to her alchemical moment. Where in your life do you employ distraction?

_____

_____

_____

What do you need from yourself in order to feel greater happiness?

_____

_____

_____

Do you make time in your life for daily spiritual practice? If not, what practices would help you to connect more consistently and deeply with Spirit/God/Creator?

_____

_____

145

_____

_____

Living in Joy

Shelley Riutta

"The natural state of your authentic self is Joy" - Shelley Riutta

*E*ver since I could remember, I'd battled an ongoing, low-level depression. In my teens and twenties, I wore a lot of black, which mirrored how I felt inside. People would comment on how serious I was all the time. I struggled to feel happiness and joy, and often wondered if I'd forgotten what they even felt like.

After graduating from college, I moved from Wisconsin to Dallas, Texas with my friend Suzie, who'd gotten a job as a buyer with Neiman Marcus. I thought a change of location and the process of landing my first "real" job would finally lift me out of my depression. But once the initial excitement of being in a new city wore off, I realized that I was no better off than I'd been before. In fact, the stress of trying to find a job in a city where I knew virtually no one was so intense that I started having panic attacks.

I had never seen a counselor before, but I knew I needed help. I still had no job and very little money, but I found a United Way-funded agency where I could see a counselor for free.

Suzanne was a tall, gentle-spirited woman. She helped me understand that my panic was the result of putting a lid on my authentic emotions—something I'd been doing for years. My move to Dallas was the catalyst for all those repressed emotions to come flooding back. As I worked with Suzanne, the panic attacks subsided, and I began for the very first time to listen for the voice of my authentic self.

147

During this time, I struggled with some big questions. What is my Life Purpose? What am I on the planet to do? My undergraduate degree was in Marketing, but after so much difficulty finding a job I wondered if I was going down the wrong path altogether.

I began to journal, meditate, run, and explore my spirituality in order to deepen the connection with my authentic self and maybe find some answers. It was one of the scariest times in my life. I was still new to Dallas, and had made hardly any new friends. The voice in my head kept saying, "What are you doing exploring like this? You just spent four years getting your degree! Get out there and look for a job in your field!" But then, softly at first, the voice of my authentic self would counter, "It's time to listen to me. I will lead you where you need to go. Please don't ignore me any longer."

As I continued to ask for guidance about my true path, messages started to come to me. "Let your passion guide you," I heard. "That passion is your authentic self speaking." When I began to reflect on what I felt passionate about, it was clear that my calling was in psychology and personal growth. Even in middle school, I was always reading my mom's self-help books—like Wayne Dyer's *The Sky's The Limit*. I had an insatiable desire to learn about people and what made them tick.

In fact, I'd started college as a psychology major but switched to marketing after people kept telling me, "You'll never make money in that field." After watching my mom struggle as a single parent, I never wanted to be in that position. Out of fear, I changed my major after my freshman year.

Now, years later, my panic attacks were helping to steer me back to my true path. Rather than keep up the futile search for a job in marketing, I decided to go home to Wisconsin and go back to school.

I enrolled in a graduate program to become a therapist. Once I was back on track, my path seemed to unfold easily. When I finished school, I easily found jobs in my field, and always seemed to know which steps to take to move forward along my path. Letting my passion be my guide, I gravitated toward a holistic approach to therapy, and began studying breathwork and Inner Systems.

Soon, I took the courageous step of opening my own Holistic Psychotherapy practice. I used everything I'd learned on my own journey to help my clients.

By 2002, everything was flourishing in my life. I had amazing friendships and a thriving, financially successful practice doing work I loved. But I was starting to feel like there was something else in store for me—something else I was meant to be doing. My depression had subsided once I tapped into my authentic self and lined up with my life purpose, but my intuition was hinting at a higher level of joy and freedom that lay just beyond where I was now.

Over the years, I'd become a pioneer in holistic methods of healing, but I would only share with my clients what truly worked. If I was going to take my clients to the next level, I had to first get there myself.

I prayed and meditated, asking for guidance along this new path. What came to me felt truly transformational. The information showed up in the form of a book called *Excuse Me, Your Life is Waiting*, by Lynn Grabhorn. This book opened my eyes to the idea that there are levels of joy, and that they are within our own choosing. Joy wasn't just a gift—it was something that could be cultivated and expanded.

This blew me away. I began experimenting on myself to see if this was really true. Sure enough, as I worked with the different exercises and techniques, I was able to feel higher levels of joy than I ever had before. I was laughing more, pursuing activities that were fun for me, and finding joy in the simplest pleasures. I then worked with expanding the length of time I could maintain these high levels of joy.

I felt like a kid who's just discovered the most magical gift ever. I was finally feeling the level of joy that I came to this planet to feel! At first, I didn't tell anyone what I was doing with this work, because I wanted to see what would happen as I grew in my own joy. Sure enough, the people close to me began to notice that I was much lighter and happier, and asked me what was different.

My next step was to bring this joy work into my practice with my private clients, and also with day-long workshops. This was around the time of the start of the Iraq war in 2003, and the energy on the planet was very heavy and dense. I was very nervous to start conducting joy workshops at a time when there was so much fear and anxiety, but when I asked for some spiritual guidance, the message I received was, "It is exactly because there is so much fear and anxiety that we want you to do this right now!"

"Living With Joy" was a huge success, and became one of my more popular workshops. Shortly after that, I led my first Joy Group, which became my "think tank" for ideas to consistently help my clients move toward and into joy.

Being able to open up to my own joy, and then being able to turn around and teach my clients how to open to theirs, has been one of the most rewarding gifts of my career, and is the foundation for what I now teach through my Holistic Therapy and Coaching Certification programs. I was so blown away by the results I'd achieved in my own life and with my clients that I wanted to train other therapists, coaches, healers, and health practitioners to do the same.

The capacity to feel joy is within our reach at any moment. No matter what is happening to us or around us, we can learn to feel it consistently and reliably. This has been the greatest lesson of my life, and it gives me great pleasure to share it with you.

Shelley discovered that her panic attacks were a symptom of her disconnection from her true path and authentic self. Have your emotions ever manifested in physical reactions?

_____

_____

_____

_____

Reaching out for help with her depression was the first step on Shelley's transformative journey. Do you need to make a change in your life? What can your first step be?

_____

_____

_____

_____

What does "living in joy" mean to you?

_____

_____

_____

Chapter
Seven

Happiness is ...
Loving Yourself

Melting the Ice Princess

Stacey Martino

I don't remember what he was saying. I don't remember how it started. All I remember is the look on Paul's face when he got out of his car in my driveway that night. I knew there was something dreadfully wrong, and I was scared it had something to do with me.

The next memory I have is of tears running down my cheeks as he told me he wanted to go back to being friends. I started sobbing—heaving, hysterical sobs.

That may sound like a perfectly normal reaction to you. After all, Paul and I had been together a long time, and it was a very serious relationship. Anyone would cry, right?

Except that I was Stacey the Ice Princess, and in the four years we were together, Paul had never seen me cry. I was cold, unfeeling. The "get it done" girl. The massive achiever. The "I'll never be hurt by anyone" girl.

Paul may have been stunned by my breakdown, but no one was more surprised than me. The voice in my head was shouting at me. "Why are you crying? You knew this was going to end eventually! What do you care? Why are you *crying*?"

My sobbing just got stronger. The self-talk in my head shifted, and turned very dark. I started hearing, "You failed. You failed. You failed." Over and over.

Not failed at the relationship—who cared about that? No, I'd failed to protect myself! That was the panic point for me. In a split second, I realized that all the protecting I had done, all the walls I'd put up, all that one-foot-in-and-one-foot-out, all that waiting for the other shoe to drop, all that keeping him out of my heart so I wouldn't get hurt ... It hadn't worked. I had failed.

I had tried for years to protect myself from this very moment, and my plan hadn't worked. I thought I'd been protecting myself from pain, but this pain was far worse than anything I had ever felt before. I was a puddle on the floor, completely broken, completely crushed. I was everything I hated in the world.

I failed. I failed. I failed.

I have never been more terrified in my life.

In that moment, I was forced to face a very unfortunate truth: you can never protect yourself from the pain of a broken heart. You can try—but what you're really doing is trying to protect yourself from the *shame*.

The timing of this life lesson was extremely unfortunate for me. My heart was split in two, but I had no plan, no protection, and no way to escape this pain. This was totally uncharted territory. I had spent my entire twenty-nine years protecting myself from being hurt by anyone. Even worse than my broken heart was my absolute terror that my world was crumbling beneath me. I didn't know how to live in a world where I couldn't protect myself from pain! I'd built my whole life around that one driving force, and in this moment, I had nothing at all to hold on to. Everything I'd thought was true was a lie, and I was unraveling.

I once heard that some people break down, while others break open. Well, that's a pretty accurate description of what happened next. I think that my deep, terrified sobs broke something open in me because, for the first time, I felt a surge of love for Paul that I had never felt before for any other human. In fact (and this may sound absurd to you), I didn't even know that a human could *feel* this kind of love!

I knew in an instant that Paul was the one I was meant to be with forever.

More terror.

"Oh my G-d, my inner voice screeched. Paul's the one I'm supposed to be with, and I've spent the last four years damaging our relationship to the point that I've ruined it, and he's leaving me!

Oh my G-d, what do I do? I don't know how to solve this. I don't have a plan for this!"

It was sheer panic. But there was one positive to hitting rock bottom: I had nothing more to lose. In that moment, I knew that whatever the risk, whatever the pain, it was worth it. The possibility of feeling that intense surge of love for Paul for the rest of my days was worth whatever pain might come.

It was worth it. *I* was worth it.

I looked up from my hysterical sobbing. From the expression of shock and terror on Paul's face, I knew that he was not experiencing the same kind of spiritual awakening that I was. He was just sitting there, stunned, with no freaking clue how to handle me—and his face clearly said, "Holy crap. This breakup couldn't be going any worse!"

I had no tools, and no relationship skills to speak of, but I was determined to turn this around. So I did the only thing I could think to do in that moment.

I begged.

I begged him to give me another chance. I told him that everything he said was right. Our relationship was crap. I was distant. I'd been playing half-assed the entire time. All of it was true. From the first day we met, I'd been protecting myself, waiting for him to end our relationship. I told him that I was heartbroken, and terrified that I'd ruined any chance we had.

I couldn't believe the things that were coming out of my mouth— but the words were flooding out of me, and I couldn't stop them. I didn't *want* to stop them.

I begged him for another chance—not for our relationship, but to be my authentic self. To figure out who I really was, and show up in our relationship as the real me. I had no idea how I was going to do that, but I was one hundred percent committed to figuring it out! "Just let me play full-assed," I said. "And then, if you don't love the *real* me, I will let you go with love. Just give me one more chance!"

I've heard Paul tell this story hundreds of times now—and every time, he tells people that in that moment, he could no longer be certain of his decision to break up with me. Before that night, he had never seen me vulnerable, raw, or open. I was suddenly a completely different Stacey, and he could no longer be sure that leaving me was the right thing to do.

So, he gave me one more chance.

We talked for fourteen hours—all through that day and into the night—and we cried the entire time. I've survived two near-death experiences, but that night with Paul, when our relationship was hanging by a thread, still tops the list as the darkest and most painful night of my life. It's also the night I'm most grateful for. It changed the entire trajectory of my life, and enabled me to become the Stacey I get to be today!

I didn't run. I didn't protect. I didn't numb or hide. I harnessed my courage, opened more, and went deeper into everything I was scared of in the world. In pure vulnerability and rawness, I walked right into my fear and made a commitment to find my way back to my most authentic self.

That night, I chose happiness.

Having been given this second chance, I devoured every book, program, and article I could find about relationships and personal development. It was not a process of becoming something I wasn't, but rather a journey back to who I really was. One day at a time, I broke down my armor, my defenses, my walls, and all the other barriers I had created in order to protect myself.

Every time I got closer to my true, authentic self, I got happier.

That said, it wasn't an easy journey. In fact, it was confusing, scary, and wildly uncomfortable most of the time. But I was committed—not to Paul, but to myself.

Like I told Paul that night, I wasn't sure that our relationship could survive. I wasn't sure that he would love the Stacey I became. But I was determined to become my best and most authentic self, no matter what.

Part of my path was learning everything I could about men, women, and relationships from every expert I could find. I learned things that shocked me—things that were the exact opposite of everything I believed before. It only made me want to dive in deeper.

My transformation had a huge impact on Paul. I was happier and more open to him, bringing the energy of the new relationship skills I was learning to our partnership. At the time, he wasn't doing any of the work I was doing—but our relationship was still transforming! We were closer, more in love, and more passionate than we had ever been.

Eventually Paul came to me and said, "Our relationship is *nothing* like it used to be. You are a completely different Stacey! You're so happy, authentic, and real. What are you reading? What are you listening to? Because I'm in!"

Together, Paul and I dove in. We worked with the greatest behaviorists, relationship experts, intimacy specialists, emotional fitness and peak psychology experts. We transformed ourselves, and ultimately created the unshakable love we share today.

Paul and I are no longer the same people we were that night on my driveway. Every day, more and more, we become our best, most authentic selves. To me, Paul Martino is the greatest man to ever walk this planet. I feel so blessed and graced by G-d to be the person he loves most in this world. Together, we have created a love and passion that far surpasses anything we ever thought possible. It's a life beyond our wildest dreams.

And to think: fourteen years ago, it was all hanging by a thread. It all could have ended, and we would have never known what a catastrophic loss it would be. Our lives together, our two beautiful children, the lives of the thousands of people we serve and *their* beautiful children ... It all could have vanished, if I hadn't had the courage, during that darkest and most painful night of my life, to stay in the pain. To open deeper, and do the work.

I think that sometimes, when people imagine choosing happiness, they think of choosing something smiley and fun—something that brings them no pain. In my experience, the moment we chose happiness is often the most painful, scary, soul-shaking moment of our lives. In order to be happy, I had to harness my courage and walk through the hell of my own fears to get to what I knew was waiting on the other side.

It all comes down to one question: is it worth it? Are *you* worth it? For me, the answer was "Yes!"

I hope it's a yes for you too.

Reflection
Questions

In what ways are you protecting, controlling, withdrawing, or putting up walls with your partner to try to protect yourself?

_____

_____

_____

_____

Where in your relationship do you avoid having raw and vulnerable conversations with your partner?

_____

_____

_____

_____

What have been the consequences of holding back?

_____

_____

_____

_____

Open Sesame

Tina van Leuven

Vivid scenes flashed before my eyes. Different settings, similar themes.

A beautiful woman dressed in royal blue and gold, managing a large estate in France and speaking up for the rights of her people. Not willing to conform to the rules, she is hunted down for her wealth. Running, running, to the edge of the cliff. She glances behind her, watching them approach—then closes her eyes, takes a deep breath, and jumps. Free and true to her Self, but wondering what might have been possible if she'd stayed in her "proper" place.

A young woman standing on a French mountainside, overlooking a magnificent landscape blurred by smoke. Tears stream down her face; she knows this is the last time she will see it. It feels too soon to say goodbye, but the choice is clear: conform, or die. She knows she won't be able to live with herself if she betrays her heart, so she takes a deep breath and starts walking down the mountain. The fire is everywhere. The heat consumes her, and her vision goes black. Free and true to her Self, but wondering what might have been possible if she'd pretended to live as they wanted her to.

The mists are parting. She has to make a choice: stay, or find him. If she stays, she might never see him again. But if she goes, she might never again set foot in her beloved homeland. Could she do it? Would he recognize her? Was it worth it? She takes a deep breath, and decides it's time for an adventure. As the mists close behind her, she tells herself not to look back. She will have to remember that the magic lives within her.

I opened my eyes and wondered if I'd been dreaming. Flashes of gold and turquoise filled my mind. Three different women, three different lives—and yet, I saw striking parallels between their experiences and the life I was living now. I envisioned a red thread running through our lives, and wondered if *this* was the moment we had all been waiting for.

I sat with my Color Oracle and asked for more information. Magnificent turquoise and gold spoke to me, reflecting perfectly the colors that had filled my mind in the wake of my vision. The message was "Open Sesame," an invitation to open myself to the wisdom that was revealing itself.

I realized that this was about claiming my "inner gold," and becoming an embodiment of divine feminine leadership. The visions were a key: it was finally time to be rid of the "conform or die" mentality and choose to live full-out, without apology. It was as if I was being summoned by my soul to come out of the mystical closet and let my authentic voice be heard without censorship of any kind.

As this information came to me, several more scenes flashed through my mind. My current life tapestry was starting to unravel, and I needed to watch it disintegrate.

I envisioned my mother, a few months pregnant with me, sitting on the table in the doctor's office. The doctor asked, "Are you aware of your husband's medical condition?" The joy she felt about having another baby was soon crushed by fear that this news might trigger my father's schizophrenia, of which she'd been entirely unaware.

To say my early years were chaotic would be an enormous understatement. I learned to walk on egg shells and not rock the boat, and became super-sensitive to what others were feeling. Somehow, I'd decided that I was the cause of my father's condition and my mum's heartache; if I just made sure to be what they wanted me to be, maybe everything would work out in the end. My people-pleaser program had been activated.

By the time I was four, my parents had divorced. My new dad entered the picture when I was five, and just after I turned thirteen my family left the Netherlands for our new home in Perth, Australia.

When I was eighteen I enrolled in massage therapy training. All of a sudden, I was surrounded by people who were drawn to the healing arts and who encouraged me to trust my intuition. I was told I had "magic hands," and it was true: I seemed to know exactly where to touch someone to release their physical symptoms and ease their emotions. And as I began to remember how to access, trust, and activate my inner resources, I got even better. My super-sensitivity was a gift after all.

Years later, I was recruited by United Airlines to fly out of Europe. It was the perfect career for my freedom-loving spirit, and challenged me to let go of the people-pleaser as I stepped into a leadership role. On one of my first flights as purser in charge of the crew, I had to confront some senior crew members. To gather the courage to speak up, I locked myself in the rest room for ten minutes while the inner gremlins had a field day. I finally decided that it didn't matter if the crew members thought I was a bitch. I had to speak truthfully, from my heart, instead of being the "nice girl," even if it would rock the boat or turn people against me. It was a major turning point in my life.

My intuitive gifts came in handy at 35,000 feet, especially after 9/11. I found myself naturally applying my spirituality and healing sciences training in practical matters. When one passenger had a panic attack, I worked my magic, and he calmed down within moments. When dealing with challenging passengers or crew members, I loved the Hawaiian Ho'oponopono prayer. I'd silently repeat, "I'm sorry, please forgive me, thank you, I love you." It worked like a charm every time!

I also became a resource for those around me in other ways. When the third client in a row came to me for career transition coaching, I knew it was time for me to make a change as well. As much as I loved the flight attendant lifestyle and the benefits of free travel, I had to pay attention to the signs. If I was going to walk my talk, it was time for a leap of faith.

At forty years old, with no savings to my name, I resigned.

I hit rock bottom in the summer of 2012. The absence of a steady paycheck triggered all the subconscious survival programs I'd been unaware of. No matter what I was doing (or not doing), nothing seemed to work. My business had come to a screeching halt. I couldn't pay my rent. Finally, a day came when I decided I had had enough. I told my soul that I was no longer willing to live like this; I'd rather just jump off a cliff and be done with it all!

That's when the visions came. Three women, choosing death and the unknown over conformity. But I didn't have to be the fourth. I could harness the power of "Open Sesame" and create something beyond my wildest dreams. I just had to let myself go.

That day, I died to my old self. For the next forty-eight hours, I wandered around in a zombie-like state, as if my inner light had gone out. I'd experienced dark times before, but this was different. I was in a void, with nothing to hold on to, and no silver lining to the cloud.

When I opened my eyes two days later, everything was different. I was later told my inner operating system had been swapped over, just like upgrading a computer. My old life was gone, and the new one was mine to create.

After twenty years of traveling, I returned home to Australia. While researching my first book, I discovered that the original meaning of "wealth" was "happiness and well-being." The accumulation of money and resources were included in the definition several centuries later.

It was a light bulb moment. Instantly, I understood that I had unconsciously been choosing happiness over money, as if it had to be one or the other. I was still believing in the old "no pain, no gain" mantra. But in reality, I was free to choose happiness *and* material fulfillment, because money follows joy.

This was what my soul had been nudging me to remember. Open Sesame had unlocked my inner treasure chest at last. I can be myself, unapologetically, and offer my gifts freely. As long as I let joy guide me every step of the way, my life will be nothing short of miraculous.

Reflection Questions

Have you ever had a vision of a past life? What did you learn from it?

_____

_____

_____

_____

Signs and symbols can be helpful tools to point out where we need to shed some light. Do you work with oracles, angel cards, or other symbolic tools? How can you incorporate these tools into your daily spiritual practice?

_____

_____

_____

_____

Sometimes, as Tina discovered, even when we're following the right path, we can unconsciously block ourselves with limiting beliefs. What ideas do you need to let go of in order to move forward with your biggest dreams?

_____

_____

_____

_____

The Path I am Strong Enough to Handle

Kellyann Schaefer

I was at the free health clinic because I didn't know where else to go.

I couldn't possibly go to my family. They wouldn't want to hear this news from me. I was supposed to be the smart one, the motivated one, the one who would go to college and "make a difference" with her life.

But I was pregnant. I mean, I *had* to be. I'd missed my period for two months in a row. So there I was, fifteen years old, sitting alone in the waiting room, surrounded by strangers, with anticipation, fear, and painful anxiety building up inside.

They called me into a little room, and a little while later, someone came in. I think he was a doctor. I remember him telling me, "You're pregnant, Kellyann."

"I'm *pregnant*?"

Even though I knew it already, there was something shocking about hearing those words. I surprised myself (and the doctor) by laughing out loud. It was weird. I was so terrified that laughing was all I could do to hold myself together.

"Yes," the doctor confirmed. "*Very* pregnant."

"What do you mean by that?" I asked, because I didn't understand what he was telling me.

He had no idea who I was. To him, I'm sure I was just another number in the line at the free clinic. Another victim of society and teenage pregnancy, another in a long line of young women destined to become nothing. And when I looked into his eyes, all I felt was shame.

"I mean, you are thirteen weeks pregnant, and you only have a couple of weeks left to make a decision."

It took me a little while to process what he was saying. I only had a couple of weeks left before I would have to decide whether or not to keep my baby.

I left the clinic with my mind whirling. Circumstances and decisions were playing out in my head like a movie, but none of them had a fairy-tale ending. What would all this mean? How could I consider keeping this child? On the other hand, how could I even consider an abortion?

I'd left my mother's house weeks before to be with my boyfriend, who was often violent. He would beat me, push me, and drag me around by the hair whenever I didn't "listen" to him. His mom and brothers also lived in the house, but they never stuck up for me. Deep down in my soul, I knew this situation was wrong for me, but I felt trapped. When I'd tried to leave him a few months before, he slit his wrists in the bathtub, saying it would be my fault if he died because he couldn't live without me. What could I do?

Despite the abuse, however, my boyfriend's house seemed the better place to go at the moment. I was a teenager, and my boyfriend swore he loved me. Plus, I was terrified to tell my mom. To tell my family. They were going to be so angry with me! I was terrified that I was going to lose their love. I could practically see my grandmothers standing over me with disgusted looks in their eyes. "You are filthy and dirty," I imagined them saying. "How dare you get yourself knocked up? How dare you ruin our hopes for you in this way?" The fear of how they might react consumed me.

It took all the strength inside me to pick up the phone and call my mom. But I knew I had to talk to her. She needed to know.

My mother was working at a pizza parlor, doing a double shift. When she came to the phone, she sounded distracted. "What is it, Kelly?"

I couldn't hold back. There was no easy way to share this news with her, or the decision I knew I was coming to in my heart. So I just blurted out three words. "I am pregnant."

"Okay. Meet me on the corner on Sunday morning, and we'll talk."

Then, she hung up. I understood: there was nothing else she could do at the moment.

In our neighborhood, abandoned houses and corner bars were as plentiful as clouds in the sky—but I knew what corner she was talking about. That short walk of less than a block felt like miles. We met outside her favorite local bar, and sat together on the big, cold cement step. My heart was heavy with dread for what I knew was coming.

I can't tell you exactly what my mom said, but it sounded something like this. "Having a baby will be a *big* mistake. You'll never go to college. You'll end up on welfare for the rest of your life. You'll end up like everybody else around here. You'll never become anything!"

I know now that she was pleading with me to choose a better future for myself—a better future than the life she lived as a single mom. But as she spoke, I realized that I had already made up my mind. There was no other option for me.

I was going to keep my baby.

I remember looking up at her, almost pleading. "I promise, mom. I'll still go to school. I'll take care of this baby, and myself, and I'll be something someday. I promise!"

When it was clear there was nothing else she could say, she hugged me, stood up, and walked away. I don't think I ever actually had her full approval—but the choice wasn't hers to make. It was mine.

Something within me changed that day. No matter what anyone else said or thought, this was *my* choice. I chose to bring my baby into the world, despite all the odds we would face together.

171

The journey that followed was incredibly difficult. I'd known it would be, but nothing could have prepared me for the challenging decisions and circumstances life sent my way. I struggled so deeply, all alone. I lost all my friends because they were still in high school, doing what "normal" fifteen-year-old kids do.

At home with my boyfriend and his family, the violence and verbal abuse continued. When I was nine months pregnant, he pushed me down the stairs. Thankfully, the baby was not harmed; that was a tragedy I wouldn't have been able to bear.

Eventually, I did leave, running from the house on a cold, dark night—hiding as I ran, for fear that he would catch me and do something terrible—because I knew now he would never change. He tormented and harassed us for more than a year, until he finally found a new girlfriend. The custody battles lasted several years more, and I never received more than a couple hundred dollars in child support. None of that mattered, though. I was safe now, and so was my daughter. I would have control over our future, not him.

I did my best to raise my beautiful baby girl in love and security, despite the odds we both faced. And in the end, it all worked out. While my family didn't help me financially, they loved me and my daughter both, and never judged me as harshly as I'd been afraid they would. I put myself through nursing school, completing my promise to myself and my mom to finish a college education. I eventually met the perfect man for me, and together we have three more children. My baby girl is now twenty-six, and getting married this year. Every time I see her big brown eyes and beautiful smile, I'm reminded of the joy she has brought not only to me, but to this world.

The choice to keep my baby was one of the hardest I've ever had to make. No teenage girl should have to go through that alone. Looking back, I'm in awe of my fifteen-year-old self: she was brave enough to choose the best version of her life that she could, even though any road she took was going to be dark and dangerous.

What I learned that day in the free clinic is that, in life, we have to make decisions. Sometimes, both choices are terrifying, and neither is something we really want. But even when either option looks negative, we still must *choose*.

To me, choosing happiness is choosing the path that I am strong enough to handle, regardless of the repercussions. At fifteen, scared and alone, I knew that keeping my child was the only choice I could live with; anything else would have killed me. Today, I see that my inner soul was calling me forward, asking me to listen to my heart despite my fears about losing the love and support of my family and friends, and surviving on my own with a child to care for and protect.

I have learned that deep inside we always know what our soul wants for us, despite what our head sometimes speaks. Now, and always, when my soul tells me to make *my* choice, I listen.

Reflection Questions

At fifteen, Kellyann had to make a choice that changed her life. What life-changing choices have you been called upon to make? What have you learned from them?

_____

_____

_____

_____

When in your life have your decisions been influenced by the opinions of others? Do you feel that these decisions were in alignment with your soul's choice?

_____

_____

_____

_____

To Kellyann, happiness is "choosing the path that I am strong enough to handle." What have you accomplished that you thought was impossible? What choices are you strong enough to face today?

_____

_____

_____

_____

Don't Mess With My Happiness!

Wendy Van de Poll

*F*or most of my life, I walked around with a deficit of love for myself.

My inner critics were powerful and convincing. They had the uncanny ability to hone in on my flaws and insecurities, and convince me, through an internal dialogue that just didn't quit, that I was incapable of being happy. With their help, I created a very challenging and unhappy life.

Even though I saw the people around me being perfectly content, loving, and successful, I didn't think I could have those things. Instead, I hated myself for all the things my inner critics told me: that I was ugly, unsuccessful, untalented, and (the worst thing in my book) incapable of loving myself.

In other words, I allowed myself to mess with my own happiness!

There were a lot of reasons why my inner critics had so much power in my life. I had a very warped view of the world, having grown up in a dysfunctional family that lived with a strict doctrine of secrets and lies. My anxiety went unmanaged for years, and I had an uncanny ability to pick friends who would ultimately drain me to the point of pain and unhappiness. I was alone, and the world was big.

Yet, as a young child, I didn't experience any of this. I was very connected to my intuition and to animals. I loved my friends (two- and four-legged) and had no concept of what unhappiness was. Up until I was twelve, talking to animals and nature spirits was part of daily life for me. It wasn't until I became a teenager that it became "uncool" to talk to animals. By creating a barrier between me and this integral part of myself, I stifled my intuition and gave the inner critics center stage.

However, that part of me that was intuitively connected did not give up on me completely. Secretly, the voices of animals crept through my visions and dreams; they attempted to help me direct my life and find a sense of self-love again, but I refused to trust them. My self-hatred was on a roll, and it was winning.

Then on March 15, 2002, I met the twelve-week-old, ten-pound ball of white fluff who would teach me more about love than anyone ever had before. Her name was Marley—or, as she came to be known, "The Divine Ms. M"—and her unbridled displays of joy and intuitive wisdom filled me again with the allure of animal connection that had been gone since my childhood.

When Marley was placed in my arms, the world around me went still and silent. I no longer heard the dogs around us barking, or the noises of the dog show where my husband Rick and I were spending the day. No longer could I hear the words of Judi, the breeder, whose unrelentingly adorable Samoyed puppies we had been oohing and aahing over a moment before.

In fact, the only thing I could hear in that moment was the swooshing of my heart and Marley's as they gushed into each other. Softly, yet powerfully, every nook and cranny of my heart was filled. We stayed like that, letting our souls fill with each other's essence, for what seemed like eternity.

And then, a thought occurred to me: is this stillness in my heart the antidote to a life without happiness?

Of course, Marley came home with us. It wasn't even a choice! And as we settled in to our new life together, I began to understand that healing my heart was the beginning of my long journey to happiness, and that Marley was here to help me.

Over the twelve years we shared together, Marley and I learned a lot about being happy. Every day, I woke up knowing that I would be looking through Marley's eyes at a world that was exciting and filled with purpose and intrigue. On our walks, she forced me to pay attention to what was important to her: a pile of fox scat, a deer trail through the woods, a bobcat peering out at us from amongst the trees.

Being brought closer to my immediate surroundings inspired the re-development of the intuitive me. By carefully capturing the details of each moment, my intuitive self was given the freedom to explore.

Every day, I awoke with the reassuring thought that Marley would not mess with my happiness. Nothing she did made me feel less than, or not good enough. With her, it was okay to just be me. I started to let my intuitive self respond to the new world that Marley was showing me. Almost without thinking about it, I found myself getting happier and happier by the day.

Marley provided me with the right balance of observation and introspection. In that way, she guided me on a path that I could not have followed on my own. Her touch on the earth became my touch. Her world became my world. Her heart was my heart.

I wish I could say that this was the end of the story, but four years ago I had a bit of a relapse, and found myself compromised both personally and professionally. On a personal level, I was staying up late, eating poorly, and falling into my old habit of letting others make decisions about how I should live my life. It felt downright creepy and weird, but I wasn't sure what to do about it. On a professional level, I was getting impatient with my clients and spending less time with them—and, as a consequence, losing business.

I was spiraling down the rabbit hole. There were days when I could barely get out of bed, let alone leave the house! Yet, Marley wouldn't leave my side.

I don't know when I finally noticed "the look," but when I did, it really got my attention. Without words, Marley let me know that I wasn't following my path to happiness. I wasn't listening to myself, or noticing the beautiful world she showed me every day. I was relying on someone else to make me happy, when I had everything I needed right here inside me.

That penetrating look from The Divine Ms. M was all that it took to snap me out of it. I got off the couch and found her leash, and let her remind me how to pay attention.

As my mind cleared, I was faced with the unrelenting reflection of the poor decisions I had been making. My inner critics were screeching—but this time, I had a partner by my side to keep me from sliding back into self-loathing.

That wasn't the only occasion that Marley helped me to realign with my path and my intuition. Over the years, I was able to rely on her again and again to show me how to play, how to enjoy the everyday—and, most importantly, how to love myself unconditionally.

But then, on December 9, 2013, I got the news that our partnership was going to end. Marley had cancer. Our veterinarian gave her a death sentence. She might only last another week or two, maybe a month, he said. In fact, he was surprised she was still alive at all.

I was devastated. What was I going to do? I was losing my best friend, teacher, partner, and guide. How was I going to survive without her? Yes, I had learned how to be happy and trust my intuitive communication skills. I'd built a practice helping others do the same. But all of that included her!

I'd seen the CAT scan, and the big honking tumor, but there was no way I was giving Marley up without a fight. The next day, Rick and I put her in the car and drove an hour to the holistic veterinarian. Armed with herbs, we began the course of alternative therapy that would keep the Divine Ms. M in our lives for another ten months.

During those last ten months of "Marley time," I had two goals. One was to do everything I could to keep her happy and comfortable. The second was to take the lessons she had taught me about how to be happy, and find a way to continue to integrate them into my life without her.

On September 22, 2014, our eyes connected as they had that day at the dog show, and Marley asked me to allow her to move on. We both knew it was time. I finally understood her lessons, and I was ready to face the world without her. Her job was complete.

For the last few hours before we went to the vet's, we held each other very close. I was numb with the thought that I would soon be losing my best friend and partner. Yet, I also carried within me an inner light. What I had gained, I could never lose again. I could make sure that I found a way to give love to myself every day, because Marley expected that of me. This was her greatest teaching for me, our promise to each other on the day we met. She gave me what no other being in my entire life had given before: unconditional love, trust, truth, and respect. The best way for me to honor her was to finally, truly, accept that gift.

As she took her last breath, I knew exactly why Marley was put into my life. She helped me learn to stand on my own. And even though she wouldn't be coming home with me again, I could choose to be happy by remembering to come home to myself.

Reflection Questions

As a teenager, Wendy blocked her own connection to animals, and opened the door to her inner critics. Are there parts of yourself that you've shut off in order to better fit in with the crowd?

_____

_____

_____

_____

What have you learned from your relationships with animals?

_____

_____

_____

_____

Wendy's gateway to self-love was learning to be present in the moment by looking through Marley's eyes. How can you become more attuned to what's happening right now, in this moment?

_____

_____

_____

_____

Afterword
EDITOR'S NOTE

*T*hree years ago, I traveled to Sedona, Arizona with a good friend and fellow yoga instructor. As sometimes happens in Sedona, without knowing quite how or why, we found ourselves in the back room of a crystal shop, seated across from a psychic reader.

As I studied the unassuming woman on the far side of a table littered with tarot cards, crystals, and not just one but several crystal skulls, I knew instantly that she was *connected*. She had something important to tell me, and I had better listen up.

The reader reached for my hand. She was tiny, but her grip was firm and reassuring. "Your daughter is here," she said.

"My who?" I didn't have a child. I had barely even considered whether I might *want* a child. But there it was again, that knowing.

"She's a beautiful spirit," the reader said. "She is filled with so much love, and she's really excited for you to be her mama. But she's patient. She'll wait until you're ready. She says ..." She paused, like she was listening. "She says, 'You need to get happy first.'"

"But I *am* happy," I said. "I mean, I think I am. Most of the time."

The reader smiled knowingly, and moved on to other topics.

I walked around in a haze for the rest of that day, and most of the next. I was going to have a daughter? And what did "get happy" mean, anyway? I thought I *was* happy. I was finally recovering from the deadly "fixer" habit that had kept me imprisoned in so many toxic relationships, and working toward a healthy, magical, stable partnership with Matthew, my amazing new fiancé. I was doing work I loved as a writer, editor, and yoga instructor. Matthew and

181

I had just moved in to a fabulous apartment on the East Side of Providence—and while he was home unpacking, I got to be here, on a yoga vacation in Sedona.

I was a very lucky girl, and I knew it.

And yet, the wise part of me had to acknowledge that I was not, actually, happy. I was still reaching for things beyond my grasp, believing that an internal feeling of support and security would eventually emerge if I accumulated enough external stuff. I still thought that I needed to present a persona of total competence at all times—that vulnerability was a weakness, and that weakness was the worst thing in the world. Most of all, I was grappling with a persistent fear of my own worthlessness. I could no longer be the "fixer," propping up unhappy people through sheer strength of will. Doing that had nearly killed me. But if I wasn't actively *doing* something for those I loved, why would they want me around?

Oh. *That's* what she meant.

As great as my life was on the outside, my thoughts about myself were hurtful, and by believing them, I was making them true. If I wanted to get happy, I needed to reframe my whole view of myself.

When I got back to Providence, I spent a lot of time walking around the city, thinking. Not meditating, precisely—just allowing my thoughts to come as they would, without censoring them. Then, one day, I reached a tentative thought tendril toward my daughter's spirit, and felt her appear, a warm glow hovering over my right shoulder.

"What's your name?" I asked her.

The message came through clear as a bell. *My name is Áine. It's spelled A-I-N-E.*

It wasn't a name that ever would have occurred to me to choose for a daughter. But it was hers, and it fit her perfectly.

"Áine," I vowed, "I am going to do my best to get happy. If I'm going to be your mom, I want to be absolutely sure that you don't learn these awful habits and thought patterns from me. I don't want you to grow up feeling not good enough, or like you have to 'earn' love by sacrificing yourself to the needs of others. I don't want you to learn to dim your light just so others don't have to see their own darkness. I don't want you to learn to apologize for who you are.

"But you're going to have to be patient with me, because I have to unlearn all of these things before I can teach you a better way."

I felt her reply. *I'll wait for you, Mama.*

Tears spilled down my cheeks. Could I actually be worthy of such trust?

For the next two years, I worked my tail off "getting happy." At first, it totally sucked. I was edgy and emotional all the time. There were so many layers of rawness under my confident, cool exterior, and I had to scratch and scrape and prod them all. But with Matthew's unwavering support and the help of an incredible circle of women friends, I was finally able to see through to the deep fears at my core, and love them away.

Then, one night, cuddled in Matthew's arms at the edge of sleep, I thought, "I'm finally happy. Truly, honestly happy. I guess it might be okay if you came now, Áine."

That night, we conceived our daughter.

For the next nine months, I dedicated my energy to growing a body for the beautiful spirit who'd waited so patiently for me to step into the light. And when at last I looked into her sparkling blue eyes, I knew that everything in my life up to this point had simply been preparing me to receive, and reciprocate, this divine, unconditional, perfect love.

As I worked with each of our incredible authors for Choosing Happiness, I found myself recalling my own journey vividly. In Stacey Martino's "Ice Princess," I saw a reflection of my former self—the girl with a solution for everything but her own untouchable heart. Shelley Lundquist's poetic prose called forth an echo of my own search for self-acceptance, and my guilt around not being able to "save" everyone who crossed my path. Mary E. Pritchard's list of perfect façades recalled to me all the various people I tried to be before I finally figured out how to just be myself.

None of us can grow in a vacuum. We learn by sharing ideas and experiences with others, and applying the truths we gather through that sharing to our own lives. The stories in this book, told with grace and raw honesty, are not intended to present to you a definitive pathway to happiness, but rather to hold up a mirror for you to see your own infinite potential.

These stories are gifts given in love, by women who have learned to love through fire and storm, through pain and desperation, through loss and redemption. By putting the words of their hearts on paper, these brave authors have committed their stories to the cause of uplifting the planet. When you employ the tools in this book to bring your most authentic, happiest self to light, their choices can become your choices. Their joy can become your joy. Their love can become your love.

It is my absolute pleasure to deliver this book into the world, and into your hands. I know you'll use it well.

As I write this Editor's Note, my beautiful baby girl is lying next to me, asleep. I marvel at the perfection of her sweet face: the expressive mouth she inherited from me, the cute elfin ears she got from her dad, and the "mystery nose" that no one can identify but which suits her perfectly nonetheless. I breathe a wish across her brow—a wish I share with you.

May you always know yourself, and love every part of your greatness.

May you trust yourself and the perfection of the gifts you bring to this world.

May you always understand that happiness is a choice, and that you are worthy to make that choice, every day.

With love,

Bryna René

Editor, Inspired Living Publishing

ABOUT OUR
Authors

Linda Bard embodies her "Hottie Sage Wise Woman" by helping multi-passionate evolutionary women around the world discover their unique Life Purpose with swiftness, clarity, and heart. She is an expert at connecting women with their souls' desires. A transformational author, inspiring speaker, and intuitive confidante, Linda also brings a rebel edge to all her programs. Find your soul's radical agreement for who you came here to be. Reach Linda at www.FindYourCreativeVoice.com and receive your complementary Soul Synergy Session!

Laura Clark, known as the Soul Wise Living Mentor, overcame decades of depression by embracing her own spirit & following her own intuition. She now teaches a unique blend of spiritual awakening tools so her clients can hear their own inner wisdom consistently, understand it more clearly, and act upon it more courageously. By doing so, they discover how to lead an inspired life filled with more joy & abundance than they ever imagined. Connect at www.SoulWiseLiving.com.

Stacey Curnow is a purpose and success coach who left behind a twenty-year career in nurse-midwifery—helping women give birth to babies—to help women (and very cool men) give birth to their big dreams. She is the founder of Midwife For Your Life, a website, blog, and series of coaching programs. Hundreds of her articles have been published in print magazines and online, and she serves clients all over the world. Visit www.StaceyCurnow.com and download your free gift, "The Purpose and Passion Guidebook."

Mal Duane is a best-selling author and Life Recovery Coach who helps women heal their broken hearts and reclaim their lives. She used her painful experience of addiction to transform her life, and now helps women discover their divine power. Mal's book, *Alpha Chick: 5 Steps for Moving from Pain to Power* is an Amazon best-seller. She has been featured on Fox News and CBS Radio, as well as MariaShriver.com, *Healthy Living*, and *Aspire Magazine*. Visit www.MalDuaneCoach.com to download your free Life Recovery Guide.

Sandi Gordon, BSc, CPC, is an author, women's empowerment and work-life balance expert, and executive coach who galvanizes people to work with passion, get the respect and love they want, and make a difference. Sandi speaks nationally on work-life balance, reducing stress and burnout, performance management, and business development, and has extensive experience with Fortune 500 corporations, mid-size businesses, and nonprofits. Learn more at www.GreatLifeBalance.com and download the free e-book, *Enough Already: 5 Surefire Strategies to Balance Your Life for Good*.

Tiffany Kane helps parents release emotional baggage so that they can be fully present with their children. Through seminars and private coaching, parents learn to embrace the perfect parent within, build confidence, eliminate self-doubt, trust themselves and have a lot more fun with their kids. Tiffany is fiercely committed to empowering parents to raise children who think creatively, communicate effectively, and take responsibility for their thoughts, words, and actions. Learn more at www.ConnectedToYourCore.com and download your free audio.

Kristi Ling is a happiness strategist and life and business coach who helps people to create a foundation for more joy, peace, self-acceptance, and love in their lives. With an extensive background in personal development, communications, and business, as well as her own compelling story of resilience and healing, Kristi is a passionate, encouraging force for positive change. You can keep up with her, read her blog, and learn about her offerings at www.KristiLing.com.

A modern-day cowgirl on a mission, *Alexa Linton* lights up her world with her infectious personality, horse sense, and her secret sauce, BodyTalk. When these forces combine, lives transform in fabulous ways! With over a decade's experience as an Equine Sport Therapist and working with thousands of pets and people, Alexa rocks a style all her own. A fire-starter by nature, it's her big mission to help women find their spark and create a life they love. Learn more at www.AlexaLinton.com.

Boni Lonnsburry is CEO of Inner Art Inc., an expert on conscious creation, and the author of the best-selling book, *The Map: To Our Responsive Universe, Where Dreams Really Do Come True*, which has won seven book awards including the prestigious Nautilus award. Boni applied the principles she teaches to transform her own life from rags to riches and loneliness to love. Her passion is teaching others to do the same. Learn more at www.LiveALifeYouLove.com and download your free Dream Building Kit.

Shelley Lundquist is an "uncovery coach" and sacred guide who uses her intuitive gifts and powerful transformational breakthrough processes to empower women in leveraging the unlimited power of their own potential. By guiding them through a journey of self-discovery and a shift in the way they perceive themselves and the world, Shelley helps each of her clients to create their best life—a peaceful, harmonious life of joy and abundance that acknowledges body, mind, and spirit. Learn more at www.LetMeMoveYou.me.

Marianne MacKenzie is a liberator of life, radically passionate about your sacred journey and bringing your desires into being. Marianne is an expert in transforming professional, executive, and entrepreneurial women into living their lives with deeper meaning, greater joy and increased purpose. "Business is a fertile arena to explore how we bring mastery to our relationships, life balance, wealth, and how we choose to express our greatest gift – our beautiful self." Learn more at www.MarianneMacKenzie.com.

187

Stacey Martino helps people who feel stuck, frustrated, and helpless with the challenges that relationship brings. Stacey firmly believes that it does not take two to tango! Her clients consistently prove that one person can transform a relationship! Through programs, events, and coaching for her Relationship Transformation System®, Stacey empowers you to create the unshakable love and unleashed passion that you really want, so you can be loved for your most authentic self! Learn more at www.LoveandPassionCoach.com.

Lynda Monk, MSW, RSW, CPCC is a Registered Social Worker, Certified Life Coach, and the founder of Creative Wellness. She regularly teaches about the healing and transformational power of writing through workshops, courses, and retreats. Lynda is the author of *Life Source Writing™: A Reflective Journaling Practice for Self-Discovery, Self-Care, Wellness and Creativity,* and coauthor of *Writing Alone Together: Journaling in a Circle of Women for Creativity, Compassion and Connection.* Visit www.CreativeWellnessWorks.com and download the Writing for Wellness Getting Started Guide.

Envisioning a world where kids crave salads, moms feel healthy and energetic, and the whole family feels fabulous after every meal, ***Mia Moran*** founded StayBasic and launched PlanSimple Mama™ and PlanSimple Meals™. A gluten-free, vegan lifestyle expert and speaker, Mia helps busy women live their best lives by making small changes that become lifelong habits—so moms no longer just survive, they *thrive*. Learn more at www.StayBasic.com and download your free meal-planning bundle.

Peggy Nolan is a sacred bad-ass warrior, vanquisher of fear, and slayer of doubt. She's a published author, yoga teacher, second-degree black belt, wife, mom, and GiGi. Peggy loves peanut butter, science fiction, beer, unicorns, dragonflies, the color purple, the beach, traveling, and naps, and is determined to be authentically creative. She lives in her empty nest in Derry, NH with her husband, Richard. Learn more at www.PeggyNolan.com.

Sangita Patel is a spiritual teacher, author, speaker, and energy healer who awakened her natural ability to heal after surviving a car accident and losing her only brother. Today, she is committed to helping those who are willing to heal themselves. She is an Integrated Energy Therapy® Master Instructor, Spring Forest Qigong Practitioner, EFT practitioner, and Teacher of Seraphic Wisdom, and specializes in coaching and healing women entrepreneurs. Learn more at www.EmbraceYourInnerSelf.com and download your free meditation, "Stress to Bliss in 5 Minutes."

Mary E. Pritchard, PhD, HHC, is the founder of the "Awakening the Goddess Within" virtual community, a Professor of Psychology at Boise State University, an esteemed blogger at *Psychology Today* and *Huffington Post*, and a frequent contributor to *Aspire Magazine*. Mary is passionate about empowering women in reconnecting with their Inner Goddesses, stepping through fear, and embracing the truth of who they are. Download your free e-workbook, "The 10 Signs Your Inner Goddess is Calling You and Tips to Answering this Sacred Call" at www.AwakeningtheGoddessWithin.net.

Consciously merging her practical tools as a licensed psychologist with her intuitive and spiritual gifts, *Debra L. Reble, PhD,* supports and empowers women to connect with their hearts and live authentically through her transformational Soul-Hearted Living™. Debra is the author of *Soul-Hearted Partnership: The Ultimate Experience of Love, Passion, and Intimacy*, a contributing author of *Inspiration for a Woman's Soul: Choosing Happiness*, and is currently working on her newest book *Being Love*. Learn more at www.DebraReble.com today.

Shelley Riutta MSE, LPC, is the founder and President of the Global Association of Holistic Psychotherapy and Coaching, and creator of a 6-Figure Holistic Psychotherapy Practice. After experiencing great success with holistic techniques in her own practice, she launched the Global Association of Holistic Psychotherapy and Coaching (GAHP) which supports Therapists, Healers, Coaches and Health Practitioners to learn more about holistic methods and develop their own 6-Figure Holistic Practices. Get your free Holistic Practice Building Kit at www.thegahp.com.

Visionary and Intuitive **Lisa Marie Rosati** is a renowned Transformation Catalyst and Magical Mentor for women. She's the Creatrix of The Goddess Lifestyle Plan™ and Sugar-Free Goddess™ and coauthor of the international best-selling books *Embracing Your Authentic Self, In Pursuit of the Divine*, and *Success In Beauty*. Lisa empowers spiritual women around the world on how to magically create an abundant life they love. www.GoddessLifestylePlan.com.

A skilled, multi-tasking mother of four, **Kellyann Schaefer** is the owner of Task Complete, a personal assistance, errand, and concierge service. Her previous career as a Registered Nurse made her adept at balancing a busy household while administering compassionate care to her patients. Today, she gives families and busy professionals reliable, compassionate assistance through educational programs, seminars, and "done for you" services, so they can meet the demands of everyday life. Learn how you can do less and live more at www.TaskComplete.com.

Wendy Van de Poll is a sought-after Animal Communication Expert, Intuitive Life Path Coach dedicated to empowering women in learning to trust their intuition by healing their blocks through the voice of animals. She is the creator of The Sacred Soul Promise Method™ and The MarleyBee Foundation™, and offers a Premier Certification Training Program in Animal Communication. Through Skype and phone Wendy provides Intuitive Life Path Sessions, Coaching, and Animal Communication sessions. Learn more at www.WendyVandePoll.com.

Tina van Leuven is the Joy Oracle at InnerDelight and author of *Money and Miracles: 40 Days to the Perfect Relationship Between Who You Are and What You Make*. She traveled the world as an international flight attendant for fifteen years while studying a wide variety of healing modalities, and now coaches passionate entrepreneurs around prioritizing themselves in their businesses and personal lives so they can do what they love without burning out. Learn more at www.InnerDelight.com.

Shann Vander Leek is a Transformation Goddess, lifelong media expert, published author, celebrated podcaster and voice over talent. She is the author of *Life on Your Terms* and coauthor of four best-selling books for women. Shann produces the Divine Feminine Spotlight and co-creates the Anxiety Slayer Podcast with over 1.5 million listens. She loves to teach women to walk in beauty and reclaim their feminine sovereignty. Visit www.TransformationGoddess.com, where women go for sacred feminine exploration.

Stacey Hoffer Weckstein is the founder of "Ignite Your Online Tribe," a sacred social media program designed to help heart-centered women entrepreneurs engage and activate their online tribes. She is also the heart and soul behind the blog www.EvolvingStacey.com, where she writes about her personal transformation—body, mind, heart, and soul. Learn more at www.StaceyHofferWeckstein.com and download Stacey's free video training, "Top 3 Social Media Mistakes Heart-Centered Female Entrepreneurs Make and What to Do Instead."

Lisa Wells specializes in helping heart-centered women entrepreneurs who feel tangled in technology simplify their online business. A Marine spouse for more than twenty-five years, she knows all too well the burdens of living a military lifestyle. The author of *Start Your Own Business as a Military Spouse Virtual Assistant*, she has a passion to support other military spouses who want to launch their own portable careers. You can find Lisa at www.LisaRWells.com.

New York Times best-selling author **Christy Whitman** has appeared on The Today Show and The Morning Show. Her work has been featured in *People Magazine*, *Seventeen*, *Woman's Day*, *Hollywood Life*, and *Teen Vogue*, among others. The CEO and founder of the Quantum Success Coaching Academy, Christy has helped thousands of people worldwide achieve their goals through empowerment seminars, coaching sessions, and products. She lives in Montreal with her husband, Frederic, and their two boys, Alexander and Maxim. Meet her at www.ChristyWhitman.com and www.TheArtofHavingItAll.com.

ABOUT THE PUBLISHER
Linda Joy

*B*est-selling inspirational publisher, Host, and Authentic Marketing and List-Building Catalyst Linda Joy is one of today's premier voices in women's inspirational publishing. Her six multimedia brands serve over 42,000 women who embrace her message of love, feminine wisdom, and self-empowerment. Ms. Joy is passionate about encouraging women to rediscover and reconnect with their inner wisdom, and empowering them to live deeper, more authentic, inspired lives both personally and professionally.

Linda is the publisher of *Aspire Magazine*, the premier inspirational magazine for women, as well as the Creatrix behind Inspired Living Publishing, through which she has created three best-selling anthologies, *Inspiration for a Woman's Soul: Choosing Happiness* (2015), *Embracing Your Authentic Self* (2011), and *A Juicy, Joyful Life* (2010). Over eighty visionary women have become best-selling authors thanks to these books and the support and expertise of Inspired Living Publishing's heart-centered team. Learn more about upcoming print and e-book publishing projects at www.InspiredLivingPublishing.com.

In her role as an Authentic Marketing and List-Building Catalyst, Linda offers high-visibility marketing, publishing, and list building programs to select heart-centered female entrepreneurs, coaches, and visionary authors. Linda's proven feminine collaborative model puts her clients' brands, messages, and wisdom in front of the women they are meant to serve while enhancing their expert status. Learn more about Linda's programs and upcoming events at www.Linda-Joy.com.

ABOUT THE EDITOR
Bryna René

*B*ryna René is an experienced editor, published author, yoga instructor, musician, photographer, and "general creative" with a passion for helping others live in greater awareness and joy. Her editing portfolio includes numerous successful non-fiction titles, including both previous Inspired Living Publishing anthologies, *A Juicy, Joyful Life* (2010) and *Embracing Your Authentic Self (2011).*

Bryna lives near Providence, Rhode Island with her husband, Matthew, and their daughter, Áine. To learn more about Bryna and her current projects, please visit www.brynarene.com and www.wordsbyaphrodite.com.